9/17

D0817999

More Teaching Kids to  Love the Earth

More Teaching Kids to Love the Earth

James Kasperson

Marina Lachecki

Illustrations by Karlyn Holman

Pfeifer-Hamilton
Duluth, Minnesota

Pfeifer-Hamilton
210 West Michigan
Duluth MN 55802-1908
218-727-0500

More Teaching Kids to Love the Earth
© 1995 by James Kasperson and Marina Lachecki. Illustrations © 1995 by Karlyn Holman. All rights reserved. Except for short excerpts for review purposes, no part of this book may be reproduced or transmitted in any form by any means, electronic or mechanical, including photocopying, without permission in writing from the publisher.

Printed in the United States of America

10   9   8   7   6   5   4   3   2   1

Editorial Director: Susan Gustafson
Art Director: Joy Morgan Dey

Library of Congress Cataloging-in-Publication Data
Lachecki, Marina.
    More teaching kids to love the earth / Marina Lachecki and James
Kasperson.
        p.   cm.
    Sequel to: Teaching kids to love the earth.
    Includes bibliographical references.
    ISBN 1-57025-040-5 : $14.95
    1. Nature study—Activity programs.   I. Kasperson, James.   II. Title.
    III. Title: Teaching kids to love the earth.
        QH54.5.L34   1994   94-4001
        508—dc20   CIP

Contents

Introduction

Is not the sky a father, and the earth a mother,
and all living things with feet and roots their children?
—Black Elk

Human beings live in relationship with the earth. We are touched by the earth in the discovery of wild strawberries or on a wade through breaking waves. We see love grow in a child's eyes as a butterfly lands on his hand. We acknowledge the gifts of the earth as gardens bloom and bear fruit. We grow old with the earth as maple saplings planted in our backyards provide support for the treehouses of our grand-children. We weep with the earth when the lakes fished in our youth no longer provide safe food.

This book is a collection of activities and stories that invite us to live in partnership with the earth. Each section explores a different concept in relating to the earth: love, trust, nurture, growth, and rec-onciliation. The stories share the variety of ways people live with the earth. The activities, other ideas, and resources extend the concepts into our homes and places of work.

We have fallen in love with the earth. Now let us live with her, with all her mysteries and moods, with all the surprises of a living relationship, with all the joy and wisdom that comes from a lifetime commitment.

Love

Love binds two lives together through experience and emotion. Love inspires, connects, and heals. It allows you to live beyond yourself and reach out to another. Love creates a dynamic of mutual response.

In this section, the stories and activities are designed to encourage a life-long love for the earth. Explore and experience the joys of the earth. Listen to its many voices and moods. Come to know the earth intimately as it draws you closer. As your history of shared experiences grows, your romance with the earth develops. Individual moments of exploration and discovery become memories to celebrate.

Live well with the earth.

Love

Come to
know
the earth
intimately.

Romance

Some people are fascinated with fish. Other people are passionate about rivers, lakes, and oceans; still others care deeply about trees, plants, or flowers.

Love for the earth develops as naturally as love between a man and a woman, between parents and children, between friends. Developing a relationship with the earth is no more difficult than developing any other loving relationship.

In the following story, Grandpa Aubrey tells his grandchildren about the first time he felt his love for the earth.

A Fish Story

As Aubrey Sloane pulled off the county trunk highway and parked near a little stone bridge, the cab of his pickup was filled with his granddaughter's voice.

"This is the wrong spot, Grandpa," Sally said as she leaned forward to see around her brother, Jeff, who was in the middle of the cab. "Last year and the year before we parked over the hill in the parking lot that the cross-country skiers use."

As Aubrey opened the door, he smiled at his granddaughter. "This is the old way into our planting spot, Sally." He took a spade out of the pickup box and handed it to Jeff. "The trail that we used for the last two years was created by the Forest Service for winter skiing, but the trail we're hiking today was the only route into this spot for many years." He handed Sally the lunch bag and reached for a potted apple sapling.

The crisp morning air was starting to surrender to a strong October sun. Aubrey motioned toward the top of a nearby hill. "We'll head to the top of that hill and then I'll lead the way for a while."

Sally ran ahead while Jeff walked along with his grandfather.

"Why do we have to walk so far to plant this tree, Grandpa?" Jeff asked as he considered carrying the spade for what looked like a long hike.

"I guess we could plant it anywhere, Jeff," Aubrey replied. "But, there's something special for me in planting on the old Prybla homestead."

"It seems crazy to me to plant all of these apple trees so far in the woods," Jeff added. "Nobody ever goes in there to eat them."

They caught up with Sally at the top of the hill. "The deer eat them," Sally responded. "Don't they, Grandpa? Don't the deer eat the apples?"

"Yes, Sally, deer and other animals eat them. Some of the apples just go back into the soil as they decompose." Aubrey took the lead now as they walked along the ridge.

"How many years have you planted trees here, Grandpa?" Jeff asked. "And why? Why go to all this work every year?"

They joined a trail that ran along the ridge. Pine and spruce trees obscured the view of the valley below.

Aubrey stopped by two round boulders that marked the splitting of the trail. He sat on one and answered Jeff. "When your grandmother was alive, we exchanged gifts each year on our wedding anniversary. We didn't pick fancy presents, but the act of giving reminded us that we loved each other. This annual planting is something like that. I do it as a gift for the earth. It's a reminder that I love being outdoors and a thanks for all the joy the earth has given me. I plant trees at the old Prybla place because it was there that I first realized how important my relationship with the earth was."

Sally, who loved a story, knew that this was her cue to ask for more. "What happened there, Grandpa?" she asked as she sat down with her back against the other rock.

"It was in October, the end of the fishing season, many years ago," Aubrey began. "I was making my annual trip to the flats down by the homestead. The native brookies seem to run bigger there in the fall.

"I only fished on Sundays because as a mail carrier I worked the other six. I packed the car the night before for only two trips each year: the first and the last. They seemed special, so connected to each other. The first celebrated the promise of a new season and the last recognized the passing of time, a few successes, and maybe the sadness of another season gone by and winter coming on.

"Well, that fall day I took just one rod, an old split bamboo rod made in Ohio, and one flybox filled with streamers that imitate minnows. During the summer the fish feed on mayflies and grasshoppers. In the fall, the big trout prefer minnows. I put all of my equipment in the truck and then made lunch for the next day. It was my traditional lunch: a braunschweiger sandwich, club crackers and cheddar cheese, an apple, and Oreos."

"Hey, that's what we have today," Sally interjected. "You mean that you always eat the same thing when you come here?"

"That's just part of the fun," Aubrey shrugged.

"Braunschweiger isn't much fun to me," Jeff grimaced.

Aubrey continued, "The morning was perfect. As I climbed the hill from the bridge where we parked today, the river was marked by a fog. The air was cold from the night before and was sending the moisture up from the warmer river water. You could trace the path of the river by the fog hovering above the tree tops. The sun soon burned off the fog, but until then the fog looked like the river extending up into the air. From the top of the hill I could see the bend that marked the beginning of the Prybla flats.

"When I reached this spot, I sat down. Do you kids know that this trail was once a main highway in this area? You know what I mean? This is the old Flambeau Trail, which was the major travel route for the Indians in northern Wisconsin. Sometimes when I walk it I almost expect to meet a party of traveling Ojibwe."

"Do they still use it, Grandpa?" Sally asked.

"Only for recreation like we do, Sally." Aubrey smiled and continued with his story.

"On that day I felt like I was not alone as I descended into the river basin. I would stop and listen. I even looked back. There was no one. But this part of the forest contained life in a special way. I still believe that. Can you feel it?" Aubrey stopped and looked around as if he were listening for something.

"I stepped up on an old foundation to watch the river for a hatch or other sign of fish. It's funny how long it takes to see into the river. First, you see the obvious — the rocks, the flows, the banks. But then the river seems to clear, to open up to your eyes. Parts of the bottom appear, even though they were always there. Shapes, branches, plants, and then fish become visible. I sit sometimes for up to a half hour. We'll stop and watch today before we plant."

"I hope not for a half hour," Jeff responded.

Aubrey laughed and continued. "I spotted a sixteen-incher that occasionally swam out from an undercut in the opposite bank. I first saw him when he slipped out over a portion of the bottom that was sunlit. A small crack of sun fell over two large granite rocks. I noticed that together the rocks looked like the head and body of a fox. Then the fish slipped into view and out again so fast that I wasn't even sure that I had seen it. I stood still and peeked just beyond the rock fox into the shadow of the other bank. There he was, feasting.

"A school of sculpin minnows was holding in a little side current six feet upstream from him—sculpin are the little black bullheads that you sometimes see. They looked like a black cloud breathing with the current. One side of the school occasionally swayed out into the main current scattering two or three sculpin struggling downstream. This trout would swim out and inhale one from each group.

"I tied on a black muddler minnow, a deerhair fly tied to imitate the sculpin. I entered the river in a crouch because behind me was blue sky, and trout can easily spot a silhouette against blue sky. I positioned myself in the middle of the river, fifteen yards from the trout. I quickly cast the fly upstream from this fish. I timed it to coincide with the next batch of stray sculpin. Before it landed, a tansy weed on the other shore seemed to reach out and grab the fly.

"I was stuck. I knew I had to either break it off or cast my fly line beyond the weed to pull it loose from behind. Either maneuver risked spooking the fish. What could I do?

"This may not surprise you. I sat down. I found a nearby rock that was showing its low-water head and sat down. To think. To wait.

"As I sat there my fly line formed a narrow little suspension bridge between me and the clearing on the other side. I listened to the sound of the river and began to forget about my predicament. I heard at least three distinct voices: a gentle bubbling, the hissing of rocks breaking the water's downhill slide, and, from somewhere in the river, a rumbling. No, it was a drumming—a deep sound that I had never heard before. It had a rhythm, but I couldn't quite get it. I tried at first and then I just listened. First I listened to each of the three voices and then to all of them together.

"Then I looked around. I saw the warm fall colors of this valley. I saw the river shooting silver reflections of the sun, interrupted by dark, root-beer stretches of flowing water."

"Did you figure out how to get your line loose, Grandpa?" Sally interrupted.

Aubrey stood up, getting ready to continue the journey to the river. "I figured out that the fish didn't matter, Sally. I realized that my line already was hooked to the trophy that I had been chasing: the earth. I realized that it wasn't catching fish that I loved all these years. I loved the earth."

Jeff looked up and asked, "What about the fish? Did you catch him?"

"I spooked him the minute I stood up. I broke the line and went home. Now come with me and let's plant that tree."

Purpose: To share your feelings of love for the earth with another person and invite them to join you in giving the earth a gift.

Participants: Preschool to lower elementary school-age children, families, and groups of adults.

Become an Earth Romantic

Setting: A forest or wooded area, a garden, or a yard.

Materials: Earth stories, a spade, and a tree sapling.

How-To: Remember a time when you felt love for the earth. It could be a memory from childhood or one from a recent outing. What were you doing at the time? What did you sense—beauty? joy? peace?

Share the memory with a child, a close friend, or a member of your family. Encourage that person to remember and tell you about a similar experience.

Think of a gift that would help you show your love for the earth. Ask the person with whom you're sharing to participate in the giving of this gift.

In this chapter's story, the grandfather annually plants a tree as a gift to the earth. If you also choose to plant a tree, the following instructions will help ensure that the tree will live and grow.

The spring and fall are both good times to plant, depending on the species of tree or shrub. To prepare the soil for the tree seedling or sapling, use the spade to dig a hole. Carefully take the sod off. Mix the remaining soil with peat, manure, or compost. This provides a mineral-rich bed for the growing tree. Remove this soil to the side of the hole. Water the hole generously. Then place the tree into the hole. Gently tamp down the soil around the sapling. Place the sod around the trunk of the sapling, watering the ground generously again. If the weather is dry, water the sapling during the first few weeks of the transplant. This care will ensure its survival.

1. Follow along as a toddler explores flowers, bugs, toads, or frogs. Let yourself be drawn into the child's delight and love for the natural world. Then begin exploring that same world yourself. Let your delight focus your attention. Let your emotions be expressed.

2. Watch the world around you. Look for birds, insects, animals, or fish. Pick one particular creature to investigate. Watch it. Read books about it. Become your family's expert on this creature. Share the magic that you discover.

3. Find your earth passion. Spend an entire year exploring a variety of outdoor activities. Then choose one that fits you. Live with that interest throughout the next year. If it's gardening, plot out a month-by-month immersion into planning, ordering seeds, sprouting seedlings, using a coldframe, turning the ground in the spring, planting, weeding, and harvesting. Make your passion a year-round activity.

4. Take someone to a special place you enjoy. Tell the person why that place is so special to you.

5. Have someone share their passion for the earth with you, whether it is bird-watching, fishing, hunting, gardening, boating, or berry picking, to name just a few. Ask questions about when they began doing the activity; do they have any rituals in doing it? are there special times of the year to observe?

6. Each year, celebrate Earth Day, April 22, by giving the earth a gift. For example, donate money to a conservation organization, plant flowers or shrubs in your backyard for wildlife, or build a bird house.

Other Ideas for Becoming an Earth Romantic

7.   Commemorate your personal anniversaries with the earth: the first fish caught, your first camping trip, the first time you saw an animal in the wild.

8.   Join an organization that fosters romance with the earth, such as the Izaak Walton League, Trout Unlimited, Sierra Club, Audubon Society, The Nature Conservancy.

Did You Know?

Did you know that in many cultures, the earth is recognized as a living being that humans can relate to as a friend?

Aubrey Sloane, the grandfather in this chapter's story, enjoyed an intimate relationship with the earth and celebrated that relationship by sharing it with his grandchildren.

The idea of being in relationship with the earth is an ancient one. Greek philosophers, for instance, taught that the earth was a living being. According to Greek mythology, the goddess of the earth, Gaia, was born when the egg laid by a great black bird, Nyx (night), hatched. The golden-winged Eros (love) emerged from the eggshell, which broke into two parts: the sky (Ouranous) and the earth (Gaia).

A twelfth-century merchant's son, Francis of Assisi, was also drawn into the beauty and mystery of relating to the natural world. He founded a monastic movement that advocated a simple lifestyle respectful of all living creatures. He and his followers addressed the sun as brother and the moon as sister.

Many nineteenth-century writers believed that human beings were a part of nature, not separate from it, and that humans needed to get back in touch with nature. These writers were part of the Romantic movement, which valued passionate living, thinking, adventure, and beauty. Romantics believed that emotions were more important than the intellect.

British writer William Wordsworth believed that humans could learn more by communing with nature than by studying books. Others believed that harmony with nature was the source of all goodness and truth. Through their writing, literary naturalists such as Emerson, Burroughs, and Thoreau shared their appreciation and interest in the natural world and their belief that the natural world could be a source of the human feelings of love and compassion.

The native peoples of North America also taught and continue to teach that humans are in relationship with other creatures on the earth, as well as the ground beneath their feet, the sky, and the water. In the mid-1850s the federal government wanted to buy lands of the Northwest Indian nations. Chief Seattle responded with words that remain an eloquent testimony to their relationship with the earth:

> My father said to me, "I know the sap that courses through the trees as I know the blood that flows in my veins. We are part of the earth and it is part of us. The perfumed flowers are our sisters. The bear, the deer, the great eagle, these are our brothers. The rocky crests, the meadows, the ponies, all belong to the same family." The voice of my ancestors said to me, "the shining water that flows in the streams and rivers is not simply water, but the blood of your grandfather's grandfather. . . . The rivers are our brothers. . . . You must give to the rivers the kindness you would give to any brother."

In 1975, an eminent atmospheric scientist, James Lovelock, joined in the tradition of Greek philosophers, Francis of Assisi, Thoreau, and Chief Seattle in calling the earth a living being. He published an article in *New Scientist* advocating a new living-earth theory known as the Gaia Hypothesis. This theory states that the primary characteristic of living organisms is their ability to organize material conditions for their survival. Based on evaluation of various systems and chemical cycles on earth, scientists provided new insight into understanding the earth as a living organism.

Throughout history, people have understood that when humans acknowledge a familial relationship with the earth, they will respect it, much as they would a family member or friend. Care and compassion are natural outgrowths of this understanding.

Resources

Brother Eagle, Sister Sky: A Message from Chief Seattle. Illustrated by Susan Jeffers. New York: Dial Books, 1991.

Meet My Psychiatrist by Les Blacklock. Bloomington, Minn.: Voyageur Press, 1977.

How Nature Works: Regenerating Kinship with Planet Earth by Michael J. Cohen. Portland, Oreg.: Stillpoint Publishing, 1988.

Gaia: A New Look at Life on Earth by James Lovelock. New York: Oxford University Press, 1979.

Sacred Places: How the Living Earth Seeks Our Friendship by James A. Swan. Sante Fe, N. M.: Bear and Company Publishing, 1990.

Teaching Kids to Love the Earth by Marina Lachecki, Joseph Passineau, Ann Linnea, and Paul Treuer. Duluth, Minn.: Pfeifer-Hamilton Publishers, 1991.

The Wisdom of the Elders: Honoring Sacred Native Visions of Nature by David Suzuki and Peter Knudson. New York: Bantam Books, 1992.

Giving: Ojibwa Stories And Legends edited by Georgia Elston. Lakefield, Ontario: Waapoone Publishing and Promotion, 1985.

Love

Come to
know
the earth
intimately.

Listening

As we live in relationship with the earth, we need to listen. The earth speaks to us all the time, in many ways and in many places. By listening, we find our lives changed and our relationship with the earth enriched. We hear its cries and are moved to action. The chuckle of a stream or the laugh of a loon delights us.

The earth speaks in many moods and tones. It roars in thunderstorm and whispers in snowfall.

In "The Sound of Snowflakes," the earth whispers to Rob, and he stops to listen.

The Sound of Snowflakes

Rob was in a windowless room when it started to snow. His attention was focused somewhere in the middle of a conference table, the second of four such tables he would sit at that day. This particular meeting focused on a potential merger of two social service agencies, one of which he represented. The work was intense. His schedule was tight. He had twenty minutes to get to his next meeting, at a location all the way across town. He was in such a hurry when he left the building that he didn't even notice the snow falling.

As Rob reached the parking lot, he realized that he was not the only one in a hurry. Three others from the meeting were already leaving. He waved as the last one passed him, then noticed a dim amber glow from the headlights of his car. It had been dark when he left home, but light when he arrived. He had left the headlights on.

He tried to start his car. First it gave a groan and then only a clicking noise. He walked back to the building, called a tow truck, and returned to the car to wait. He brushed two inches of snow off the car, then walked to the edge of the parking lot. There he cleared the snow off a short post and sat down, facing the nearby freeway. From this spot he could signal to the tow truck as it came down the exit.

The snow fell straight down. Rob noticed the solid whiteness of the fallen snow—the street was white, the parking lot was white, even the sloped roof of a nearby church was white—compared to the broken white pattern of the falling snow.

As a car drove by, he realized the usual noise was muffled. The snow dulled all sounds. As the car drove out of sight, he kept listening intently. He wondered if each flake made a sound as it landed on a surface. He listened and heard a silence, soft and full. The soundless arrival of another winter.

As the flakes became larger, Rob began watching them arrive on the ground. Each flake appeared to defy gravity, not falling but floating downward, slowly and purposefully, toward an intentional landing. They landed with a gentle stop. Rob watched closely as the flakes grew to nearly the size of a quarter.

He tilted his head upward and squinted. He felt as if he were rising, floating upward in a solution of white particles.

He closed his eyes and felt the snow land on his cheeks. First there was a sting and then a bit of wetness. He stuck out his tongue. The snow felt cold and dry against his warm, wet tongue.

Rob remembered that when he was a child he often played in the snow until his pants were frozen stiff. He remembered snowmen and snowball fights. He remembered being snowbound at his cousin's house for three days.

For the first time in days, Rob was sitting still and feeling happy. The snow was speaking to him. He was listening.

Listen to the Earth

Purpose: To listen to the earth's many voices as it speaks to us.

Participants: All ages.

Setting: Any spot outdoors that allows a person to safely sit down.

Materials: Paper and a pencil or pen.

How-To: Before going outside each participant should list on the left-hand side of each page the words *eyes, ears, nose, mouth, skin, body, mood,* and *message.*

All the participants should sit together silently in the same general area. After a few minutes of getting used to the spot, they should focus on each of their senses. What is the earth telling me through my eyes? my nose? my skin? It may be a simple message like, "Go inside, it's too cold out here."

As their sensations become clear, ask participants to record them and then to suggest the mood from which the earth is speaking and record the specific message that the earth has for them on that day.

When the group gathers again, share the moods and the messages. Are they consistent? Do the observations tell us about the earth or the participant? Repeat this activity on three successive days in the same spot and compare people's perceptions from day to day. Did they hear the same thing? Did the earth have a different message? Were they listening to a variety of the earth's many voices?

Other Ideas for Listening to the Earth

1. Take your family or group of friends to a park. Pair off and take turns being blindfolded. Move to several spots as you listen, noting what you hear. Attempt to isolate four or five different sounds. Share the results of your exploration with the rest of the group. Try the same activity in your backyard or in a field or forest. Make a sound test a few times every week.

2. Be an ear detective. Take a portable recorder outside. Record for fifteen minutes, then listen as you play the tape. Do you hear any sounds on the tape that you didn't notice as you were recording? Often our ears edit out sounds.

3. Try this old exercise. When a storm brings thunder and lightning, get out a stopwatch or a watch that notes seconds. Start counting at the sight of the lightning bolt and stop at the sound of thunder. Divide the number of seconds by five and you will know the number of miles away that the lightning was.

4. What season is it? What are the plants and animals doing? What is the mood of the season? Reflect on the season of the year and the seasons of your life.

5. Ask your neighbors about predictable local weather patterns and regional weather lore. Do people say, for instance, "The

wind changes every day between 12:30 and 1:00 P.M."; or "If there is a ring around the moon, it will rain within twenty-four hours."? Make a list of these predictions for your area and check their accuracy over the course of a year.

6. Set up a home weather station to monitor changes in the weather. Instruments may include an indoor/outdoor thermometer, a rain gauge, a barometer, a weather vane, a wind speed indicator, and a log to record the data.

7. Listen to the music of the earth. While walking through the woods, figure out what birds, animals, or insects make sounds that remind you of strings, horns, drums, or harps.

8. Play the owl ear game. Owls detect their prey with both their eyes and their ears. From a group of friends, choose one person to be a mouse and make squeaking sounds. Choose two others to be owl ears. Blindfold both of these individuals, having one stand up and one sit on a chair close by. This positioning simulates the placement of the ears on an owl. Then, with the mouse-person squeaking, have the blindfolded owl-persons try to locate the sound.

9. Notice the sounds of the areas through which you travel on a family vacation. List the sounds that you don't hear at home.

10. Be a mystery animal. Arrange a group of children in a circle. Progress around the circle, with each child taking a turn imitating the sound of an animal or bird. Other members of the circle attempt to guess what the animal or bird is.

Did You Know?

Did you know that animals with an acute sense of hearing often have large ears? As Rob stopped in the middle of a busy day and listened to the stillness of falling snow, like the deer, the field mouse, and the rabbit, he used his ears to experience the world around him. Humans don't have especially large ears, but careful listening can help us understand the world around us.

If you watch dogs closely, you'll notice that they move their ears to pinpoint sound. Most people have only one muscle to move their ears, but dogs have seventeen. Often, an animal's survival depends on hearing. For them, hearing is their most valuable sense.

How do ears work? The outer ear collects the sounds, causing the ear drum to vibrate. The middle ear amplifies the vibrations, which the inner ear receives and sends as a message to the brain. Because the hearing of humans is not very acute, a variety of amplifying devices have been developed to enable us to hear better.

People who listen to the earth professionally are called seismologists. They listen for tremors inside the earth with a variety of sophisticated instruments, but the seismograph is their basic tool. Seismographs are located throughout the world, from Asia to South America to Europe to the United States. The seismograph, an extremely sensitive instrument, uses a stylus to record the earth's movements as lines on paper. If there are no movements, the line is straight. Minor tremors appear as wavy lines; major tremors produce large strokes. This data is then measured against a scale developed in 1935 by American seismologist Charles F. Richter.

Animals collect sounds and then interpret them. Is a predator near? Should protective cover be sought? Seismologists also interpret the data from seismographs. They compare the readings to historical patterns and alert people living near a tremor to be prepared to move in case of an earthquake.

Native Americans learned to listen to the earth, not just for protection but to enhance their lives. They spent many hours in the woods, near rivers, and in the mountains observing and listening to the natural world. They listened by noting patterns of weather, animal behavior, and the way the plant world developed. They believed every part of the natural world had a gift for humankind. Each plant had a medicine or food to share. They discovered these uses by listening to the natural world with all of their senses.

Because they intimately knew the behavior of animals, they understood when an animal crossing their path or flying overhead might be a message-bearer. If an animal exhibited unusual behavior, or stopped and looked them straight in the eye, native people believed a message was being given to them by the Great Spirit. To interpret the message, they reflected on the encounter over the next few days or weeks.

Each animal symbolized a certain ideal to be sought or attained: the hawk brought a message of foresight; the eagle, courage; the loon, fidelity; the bear, introspection; the moose, strength; the wolf, guardianship; the beaver, resourcefulness; the sturgeon, depth. By coming to understand the message the animal brought, native people were able to understand their responsibility as creatures of the earth.

Resources

Listen to Nature by Joseph Cornell. Nevada City, Calif: Dawn Publications, 1987.

Pilgrim At Tinker's Creek by Annie Dillard. New York: Bantam Books, 1974.

Sand County Almanac by Aldo Leopold. New York: Ballantine Books, 1970.

The Earth Speaks edited by Steve Van Matre and Bill Weiler. Warrenville, Ill: The Institute for Earth Education, 1983.

The Way to Start A Day by Byrd Baylor. New York: Charles Scribner's Sons, 1978.

The Other Way to Listen by Byrd Baylor. New York: Charles Scribner's Sons, 1978.

Thirteen Moons on Turtle's Back by Joseph Bruchac and Jonathon London. Illustrated by Thomas Locker. New York: Philomel Books, 1992.

Nature With Children of All Ages by Edith A. Sisson. Englewood Cliffs, N.J.: Prentice-Hall, 1982.

Love

Come to
know
the earth
intimately.

Celebration

Christmas, The Fourth of July, Thanksgiving—on these holidays, family and friends gather to commemorate historical events. People also celebrate milestones in their own lives—birthdays, anniversaries, and graduations.

Since ancient times people have also celebrated their relationship with the earth. Sun dances, equinox observations, midsummer festivals, and days to bless the harvest are all celebrations of our life with the earth.

Follow the Powwow People as they celebrate the wild rice harvest; then join in the fun. Celebrate the earth.

Powwow People

An evening wind created cat's-paws on the still waterways of the Kakagon Slough. Eli heard the reeds swishing in the wind and felt the light breeze move through his long black hair. The purple-black plumes of the wild rice swayed, dangling seeds over the dark water. Quiet lay over the sloughs, ancient home of the Anishinabe. A vision had led Eli's people there, a vision which told them to travel toward the setting sun until they came to a land where food grew on the water.

Food. That was what was on Eli's mind as he moved the canoe forward with a push of the pole. A rhythmic thumping interrupted the shushing sound of the rice brushing against the aluminum sides of the canoe. His Uncle Ronnie knelt in the front of the canoe, pulling an armful of rice plants over the canoe and then swinging a short bat down sharply on the plants to knock the grain of the wild rice into the growing pile in the bottom of the canoe. Swish, he would pull. Thump, he would pound, and the grain would tinkle as it landed in the boat.

When Ronnie stopped pounding, Eli planted the pole on the lake bottom, pushed, and moved to more rice-laden plants. It was a rhythm of the season. They had been at it for ten days now, and Eli, tired and a bit bored, was ready to celebrate the last of the harvest. That would be soon.

Tonight the powwow to celebrate the harvest would begin. It was Eli's favorite part of the fall. The food, the visitors, and the sounds of celebration all seemed to make some sense out of this task, which often seemed monotonous to an eleven-year-old like Eli. He imagined that his mother, Asabun, was cooking right now. Just a few more yards. Swish. Thump. Tinkle.

Finally Ronnie turned around. "Time to head in." He leaned back against the day's pile of wild rice and grinned at Eli. "We've got a party to go to."

Eli poled fast now, heading toward the landing. Over the ridge, the deep call of the drums could be heard. The people were gathering at summer's end to celebrate the gift of manomin, wild rice.

Asabun was busy in her home, making corn soup and fry bread for the feast. Her two youngest boys were outside, playing with cousins. Her brother Ronnie would bring Eli, her oldest son, home soon. Her daughter, Cheryl, was in her room, sewing the last piece of ribbon on her jingle dress. She would dance in the powwow tonight with her mother.

As the soup simmered, Asabun began to dress. She grasped a piece of the maroon wool of her dress between her fingers. She ran her hand along a seam and savored the crisp, gentle scratchiness of the fabric. These were times worth the waiting, times when she knew clearly who she was. The dress was trimmed with blue ribbons and shells, the identifying marks of her clan. The Bear Clan. Plant people. They were known for their knowledge of the plant world. She had been learning about the medicinal uses of roots, bark, and leaves for the past six years. She listened to the elders during spring ceremonies and at other times when they gathered to tell stories and to pass on the tradition of her people.

Asabun collected the ankle bands trimmed with bells for her sons. They, too, would dance in the powwow tonight. As she moved to the door to call her young sons, Ronnie's pickup pulled into the driveway. As Eli jumped out, Ronnie backed out of the driveway, giving a short beep of the horn, marking both hello and goodbye.

"He's in a hurry, Mom," Eli said as he slipped by her and into the house. "He's supposed to drum tonight and it sounds like things are already starting."

"Carl and Jack, come quickly," Asabun called from her front door. "I hear the drummers."

A few minutes later the family slipped out the back door, Eli first, followed by Asabun and the younger kids. As they followed a path through a small wooded area, the arbor of the powwow grounds was filling with drum groups. There would be about ten groups this first night, and more would come for Saturday's powwow.

"Is that the Bad River drummers, Mom?" Carl called.

"Yes, they always start their home powwow," Asabun answered. "Look for your Uncle Ronnie," she told the two youngest kids. "He should be drumming already."

As they walked past the edge of the parking lot, Carl pointed at a red van. "Look, there are South Dakota license plates. Let's see who else is here." Jack and Carl ran through the lot, racing to find another out-of-state license.

Jack called out first, "Here's Ontario. Minnesota and Michigan plates don't count. They're too close to home."

Carl, who had just found both, called back, "They're from out of Wisconsin. That's all that counts."

As Asabun turned away from this exchange between her two youngest children, she considered the Powwow People. That is what she called the extended family now gathered for the celebration. Many of them traveled every weekend of the summer to dance in honor of the earth, to celebrate the summer sun and the autumn harvest.

As she, Eli, and Cheryl walked through the campground, children ran from campsite to campsite. Over one hundred families were scattered throughout the meadow. Canvas and backpacker tents, camper trucks, and pop-up trailers formed a circle around the arbor. Blue tarpaulin roofs marked the community kitchens.

Asabun noticed Eli holding his shoulders back and standing taller, looking older, as they approached the circle. Boom. Boom. Boom. While a few drummers were warming up, the high-pitched voices of singers pierced the night air. Other drummers huddled around the singers, a few held tape recorders used to take new songs home to their own reservations. A lone singer chanted a phrase, followed by a chorus of voices repeating his song.

Eli breathed deeply in order to enjoy the promise of the banquet which filled the air. Bells and drums sounded as dancers took their places for the Grand Entry. A young grass-skirted dancer held the

eagle flag. He wore a shield of bones down his chest. A bustle of feathers covered his back. An elder of the tribe, wearing traditional buckskin leggings and shirt, held the American flag. He was a veteran of World War II. It was his honor to carry his country's flag in the opening ceremony and prayer.

A man walked up to the microphone. He wore a full headdress of eagle feathers and a calico red shirt with blue ribbons streaming down his chest. He spoke in his native tongue. Asabun and her family listened. She was being taught Ojibwe by a grandmother and could understand much of what he said. Eli and Cheryl could not understand, but bowed their heads in respect. It was a prayer to all the directions, to the earth, and to the Creator. A prayer of thanks for the harvest. A prayer of praise for the beauty of the earth. A prayer of promise for their future together with all of creation.

Then the drumming began. More than one hundred dancers followed the flags. They circled the arbor of drummers. The men walked in first. Soon Eli would dance with the men, but today he came in with his mother and the other women and children. All the dancers joined in the song. As the flags were planted in the ground, the dancers faced the center of the circle, dancing in place to the sound of the drums. Their knees bent with the down-beat of the drums. This was the heartbeat of the nation, their bodies pulsating with the heartbeat of the earth.

Between dances, Asabun talked with old friends. They shared experiences from the winter, when they were not able to see one another. Her younger children, bored with such conversation, ran off to join other children. The visiting, feasting, and dancing would go on long into the night.

Eli stood and watched his Uncle Ronnie and the other drummers. As Ronnie swung his arm, Eli remembered the last ten days. Thump. Swish. Tinkle. It all fit together for him: the rice falling into the canoe, hard and cold like the new winter air that was blowing; the drums that pulled Eli's heart and mind toward the circle, though his feet stood still; the people he knew, the people from other places; the food; the feathers, ribbons, bones, and shells. They were all a part of the gift of manomin. He thought of how long the harvest had seemed. Now he already looked forward to next year.

A single voice pierced the sky. The song was strong within him. It called to the dancers to return to the circle. It called others who did not have a costume to come to the circle. The drumstick pounded the drum sharply, and the sound echoed in the hearts of those dancing around the arbor.

Asabun started to sing quietly. Other women joined the song as they danced. They were not singing to one another. They were singing with the earth. They were singing from a place deep within, a place called to by the drum. Their song echoed the sound of the drum. All dancers now faced the drum, their bodies dancing to the rhythm of the drum beat. The singers called to them. The song wove its way through the dancers like the wind over the water. Asabun did not see the crowds anymore. She did not feel the women and children next to her. Her spirit traveled from the earth to the sky. She was now a part of something that was so large. Powwow People. Anishinabe. Creatures of the earth and the Creator.

Celebrate the Earth

Purpose: To participate in a celebration of the earth.

Participants: Families and friends of all ages.

Setting: Any outdoor setting.

Materials: Depends on the festival — appropriate outdoor clothing, seasonal food, and games.

How-To: Look at the variety of earth festivals celebrated around the world that are listed in the accompanying "Did You Know?" and "Resources." Check in the local newspaper or with the chamber of commerce for ethnic festivals or Native American pow-wows that may be held in your area.

Celebrations may be from a country you'd like to visit, from your ethnic heritage or community, or of your own invention.

Discover the origin or legends behind the celebration. What earth event is being celebrated? Are traditional stories, rituals, or games being shared?

If you are designing your own earth festival, use a story, song, play, or puppet show to share the celebration. Think about outdoor games you would like to play at the celebration. Discuss what food, dress, art projects, and other rituals might be appropriate for this day.

Invite family, friends, and neighbors. Celebrate the earth in a spirit of joy.

1. Read *I'm in Charge of Celebrations* by Byrd Baylor. Watch for days when something out of the ordinary happens in the natural world (a triple rainbow, a flock of unusual birds, an early snow, the first crocus in the garden). Plan a celebration. Mark your calendar and observe it again the next year. It's your personal natural holiday.

2. Celebrate Christmas with the creatures of the earth. Following the custom of European peasants, trim outdoor trees with cranberries, peanut butter pinecones, and popcorn strings. Place sheaves of wheat or other grains on your porch to feed the birds.

3. Join in the Earth Day festivities of your community. If none has been planned for April 22, organize a celebration. Dream of parades, speakers, music, food, and rituals. Then make it happen.

4. Plan a Halloween party for the neighborhood. Suggest that guests costume themselves as animals or plants.

5. Intentionally mark the entrance of a season by gathering friends and family. Decorate the house with symbols of the season (falling leaves, snowflakes, spring flowers, the sun). Plan an outing and use all five senses to experience the season. Watch the sun go down on summer solstice. Wait for the dawn on the first day of spring.

6. When the last of the garden is harvested, invite neighbors for a feast. Everyone is asked to contribute something they have either grown, made, gathered, or caught.

Other Ideas for Celebrating the Earth

7. Opening day of any fishing or hunting season is a day of celebration. Recognize not only the sport but the gift you receive.

8. Immerse yourself in a child's delight at the first snowfall. Go sledding, build snow people, have a snowball fight. Resist the temptation to shovel.

9. Celebrate the return of migrating birds. On sighting the first robin or Canada goose, note the date and compare your firsts with those of others in your community.

10. Intentionally note the earth connections of other festivals that you and your family celebrate (for example, the midwinter aspect of Christmas and the spring awakening of Easter).

Did You Know?

Did you know that sun dances and harvest festivals are celebrations of the earth? People who live close to the earth and recognize their dependence on its bounty celebrate and honor the gift of life on this planet in seasonal festivals. The Manomin festival recognizes the Ojibwe people's dependence on the earth's gift of wild rice.

There are four great earth festivals: the spring and fall equinoxes (in the northern hemisphere, March 21, spring, and September 22, fall) and the summer and winter solstices (in the northern hemisphere, June 21, summer, and December 21, winter). Equinox means equal day and night, when the sun is directly above the equator during the earth's rotation. The solstices mark times when the north pole is closest to the sun (summer in the northern hemisphere) or farthest away (winter in the northern hemisphere). The movement of the earth and sun and the resulting changes in the plant and animal worlds have for centuries been a source of fascination and celebration for humans.

The return of spring marks another time of festivities for people of the earth. British and German emigrants to America predicted spring's arrival by observing groundhogs. The groundhog, or woodchuck, is the largest member of the squirrel family. It spends its winters burrowed into the banks of creeks or brushy ravines. As the weather gets milder, groundhogs come out of hibernation. If February 2, Groundhog Day, is sunny and the groundhog sees its shadow, it is said to hurry back into its burrow, thereby predicting another six weeks of winter. That would mark the return of spring about the end of March, near the spring equinox.

For some people, Easter marks the return of life to the earth. Though it is a Christian holiday, its symbols draw upon the signs of fertility, of life renewing itself. The word *Easter* comes from Eoster, the name of the Teutonic goddess of fertility. Eggs, symbols of birth and rebirth, are decorated by people of many cultures. Some Native American tribes and the peoples of Polynesia, India, Iran, Indonesia, Greece, Latvia, Estonia, and Finland all have creation myths that depict the birth of the earth from an egg. The butterfly emerging from its winter cocoon is another symbol of life bursting forth during the springtime. For Egyptians, the rabbit was a symbol of fertility and spring—and Americans delight in the Easter bunny.

Butterflies, eggs, and rabbits are not the only natural phenomena celebrated by humans. In Japan, the strength and perseverance of the carp as it swims upstream to lay its eggs are observed in a festival of kites called Kodomo-no-Hi. This early May festival features large, colorful, and graceful kites, many shaped like carp, filling the sky. In Israel, tree-planting ceremonies honor the gift of land. Boys and girls parade through towns with spades, hoes, and watering cans. They march to nearby fields to plant trees. A similar festival, called Arbor Day, is celebrated in the United States. Iran's national holiday, No-ruz, is celebrated on the vernal equinox, March 21. One tradition calls for families to scatter wheat, celery, or lentil seeds in a bowl of water. The seeds sprout and are put in clay jugs or dishes. The plants have a special place of honor in the house during these spring festivities, for they symbolize new life and growth.

As our civilized lifestyles have moved us further away from the daily rhythms of the earth, our festivals have become less earth-centered and more human-focused. On April 22, 1970, a renewal of interest in celebrating the earth took place with the first Earth Day. It was a day of parades and projects that encouraged participants to rejoice in the beauty of the earth and to become aware of its problems. Over twenty years later, traditional feasts and celebrations are gaining popularity. Earth days are organized in hundreds of communities around the world.

So, rejoice in the earth's beauty and honor your relationship with the earth by celebrating its gifts of life.

Resources

The Sacred Harvest: Ojibway Wild Rice Gathering by Gordon Regguinti. Minneapolis, Minn.: Lerner Publications Company, 1992.

Earth Festivals by Delores L. Chapelle and Janet Bourque. Silverton, Colo.: Finn Hill Arts, 1973.

The Children's Year by Stephanie Cooper, Christine Fynes-Clinton, and Marye Rowling. Stroud, United Kingdom: Hawthorne Press, 1986.

I'm in Charge of Celebrations by Byrd Baylor and Peter Parnall. New York: Charles Scribner's Sons, 1986.

Sun Calendar by Una Jacobs. Morristown, N.J.: Silver Burdett Company, 1983.

Wildlife's Holiday Album edited by Alma Deane MacConomy. Washington, D.C.: National Wildlife Federation, 1978.

Nature Day and Night by Richard Adams. Illustrated by David Goddard. New York: Viking Press, 1978.

Kerlyn Holman

Love

Come to
know
the earth
intimately.

Intimacy

Many of us walk through life with only a casual knowledge of the people and places around us. But sometimes we experience the joy of knowing more intimately. Intimacy brings special fulfillment.

Naturalists spend their lives getting to know the earth more intimately. They anticipate the return of redpolls in the spring or the arrival of desert thunderstorms. With intimate knowledge, they know what to expect from the earth.

Through the gift of a naturalist's journal, Katie and Michael learn about their new homestead. Read the story and become more intimate with the earth around you.

Welcome Home

"We've got ourselves a fine-looking house, Katie," Michael said as he put his hands on his wife's shoulders.

They were moving into a new house in the woods, a house now filled with an assortment of cardboard boxes, plastic-draped furniture, trunks, and suitcases. It was Saturday morning, and they only had the weekend to organize the house before beginning new jobs on Monday.

Katie had never lived far from the farm on which she grew up. She would miss being close to that place. The family pond she swam in as a child was still a source of summer fun for her two boys. Katie knew every inch of the creek that ran alongside the southeast corner of their cornfield. She knew the individual personalities of over eighty cows that were the source of both family pride and income.

But now she had to begin the task of putting this new house in order and learning to live in this new place. Katie walked into the solarium. She had been drawn to this room since they first viewed the home. She imagined herself snuggled up on a couch with a cup of hot chocolate on a winter's day. The room faced south, and floor-to-ceiling windows brought streams of light and warmth into the space. She began to unpack and think about future lazy Sunday afternoons spent reading in the winter sun. Her daydream was interrupted by the streak of her boys running past the windows and into the nearby woods.

"Let them run free for now," Katie mused. "I'll tap into that boundless energy after Michael and I haul their boxes into their bedrooms."

As Katie got up to leave the solarium, she noticed a book tucked away on the windowsill. The previous owners must have forgotten this book, Katie thought. The book was well used, with turned-up corners and a coffee ring on the front. She picked it up and turned to the inside cover to see if a name could be found. Instead, she found a note.

Dear Friends,

Welcome to your new home. My husband and I began building this house over twelve years ago. It was our dream and we labored over eight of those years to complete the house you will soon call home.

Early in that adventure, I started to notice what was outside this structure. Many a day I sat on the front porch watching the black-

capped chickadees and red-breasted nuthatches take turns at the bird feeder. I was surprised by toads and garden snakes as I turned over the soil for planting in the spring. I tried to predict the time of the first rain and the first snowfall.

My favorite activity of all was to walk in the nearby woods to see which wildflowers were in bloom. I must admit I got pretty good at remembering which flowers bloomed first and in what order. They were all old friends to me.

All this and more are recorded in this journal. I wanted to take the book with me as I left this land I loved. But somehow it didn't seem right. The book is the history of this piece of earth. You are now keepers of this land and this book. I think you'll find the land to be quite a gift.

Katie opened the book. There was a page for every day of the year. Some pages were blank and some were almost filled.

May 25, 1990

I saw a tiny fawn on the road today. When it saw us, it went into the woods and sank low. Such instinct.

September 13, 1985

A family of four raccoons was seen scurrying into the old ash tree as we drove home from a concert. They went up the trunk and into the hollowed-out top.

October 14, 1986

Snow flurries turned into the first snow. Hurray.

Katie looked across the page. The journal recorded that the first snow came on this same date, October 14, from 1989 to 1992. She turned another page. The first snows in 1983, 1985, and 1988 were a week later. This was amazing. She had discovered a *Farmer's Almanac* for this piece of property.

"Katie, I need some help with this box." A large thud and call for help drew Katie back to the task at hand.

"Coming," Katie called as she ran to the kitchen. Michael stood holding a box of pots and pans, with no place to put them down.

"Michael, look what I've found," she motioned. "It's a book the owner left behind for us."

"Is it a guide for finding a place of rest for a beleaguered mover?" he quipped.

"Michael, read this note," Katie continued. "It's written to our family. The owner left a journal that contains all sorts of information about what happens outside this house."

Michael became interested and started to skim the pages.

March 20, 1989

Nine A.M. A lone coyote howled, yipped, then barked for twenty to thirty minutes. Very eerie. My sister and I went out back, thinking it may be wounded. What we discovered was a young deer that had been killed during the night. It looked as if it had been surprised in its bed.

January 8, 1990

Thousands of tiny black specks that moved around the base of an oak tree covered the nearby ski trails. I found out they are insects called springtails.

There was no more room on the April 25 page. Every inch of space, both the lines and the margins, was filled with information. On this date, the cattails were puffing out, the first leaves opened on the cherry tree, the watery call of the cowbird was heard as it sat on the birdfeeder, wood anemones and sweet coltsfoot bloomed, and in 1990 it was ninety degrees outside.

At that moment, their two boys burst through the back door.

"Mom, Dad, you have to come see this," they shouted, trying to catch their breath.

They grabbed their parents' hands and started dragging them outside.

"What's going on?" Katie called.

"You'll never guess what we saw," the oldest said, puffing.

"There's a big animal with a bandit's mask climbing an old tree," the younger brother strained to get out.

Katie looked at Michael. "Better get the journal. I think it's time we added a little history to it."

Become Intimate with the Earth

Purpose: To develop intimacy with the earth by recording the natural events that happen in specific places.

Participants: Children with the ability to write or draw. Ages five and up work best.

Setting: A city park, your backyard, or a nearby woodlot.

Materials: A sturdy notebook, field guides, and a pen or pencil.

Select a place for its convenience. For ideal records, you need to observe the plant or animal activity every one to three days. Think about your home, a park on the way to school, or a place where you take a walk frequently.

Anything that changes with the seasons and piques your interest can provide the first notes for your journal: the arrival of songbirds in the spring, the advance of wildflowers, the first ripe tomato from the garden, the first rain or snowfall.

Begin by jotting down things that are easily noticeable: the first bloom of a dandelion, animal tracks after a spring rain, aspen and cottonwood trees spreading pollen into the air. Note the date, time of day, and a comment or two on what you have observed. If you don't know the name of something, describe it or use a field guide for identification.

Pick a number of seasonal events to observe: when maple trees are tapped in late winter, when the lilac blooms, when the chickadee changes to its spring call, when the autumn leaves are in full color.

Try to observe the same event year after year. Develop a history of natural phenomena for this particular piece of land.

1. Make a wildlife or habitat map of your yard or neighborhood. Draw trees, flower beds, buildings, grassy areas, woodlots. Get to know where pigeons and robins nest, where squirrels stash their winter food, where woodpeckers hammer in search for insects.

Other Ideas for Becoming Intimate with the Earth

2. Discover the tiny world of insects. Find an anthill, or better yet, let the ants find you. Have a picnic and they will be there. See what they do with tidbits of food they find.

3. Chart the advance of spring or fall. Talk together as a family or group of friends about all the signs of spring (blooming wildflowers, nesting birds, the first rain, the first lawn mowing) or fall (the first frost, the emergence of fall color, the first ripe tomato, migrating geese). List these signs across the top of the chart, and along the side place calendar dates. Keep track of these signs and their dates from year to year.

4. As you take your morning run or walk, notice what is going on outside. Keep notes on the daily changes you see in the landscape, whether the changes are in plant or animal life.

5. Photograph a favorite tree in each season over a number of years. Record the changes in its girth. Notice who uses the tree (insects, birds, squirrels, humans).

6. Stand or sit outside in a warm-weather rainstorm. Stay long enough to get beyond feelings of discomfort. Being wet in the outdoors allows you to be vulnerable and connected to the environment in a way that is impossible in our usual dry, protected state. Do this rainy-day activity alone or share the experience with a group.

7. Sleep outside without a tent. Watch the day come to a close, watch the first stars come out, and, if you are awake, greet the dawn.

8. Blindfold a friend and lead them to a tree. Have them touch the tree and explore it using only their fingers and sense of

smell. Then take them far enough away to make them lose track of which tree they touched. Take off the blindfold and see if they can lead you to the special tree. Switch roles and try the experiment again. Talk about how you each recognized the tree you had come to know by touch.

9. Sit outside your office, school, or home with a sketch pad and a pencil. Find something to draw. Study the details of the object. Pay more attention to the object that you are drawing than to the results of your work. You are sketching in order to know the object more intimately rather than to produce art. Relax. Let your pencil lead your eyes into the intimate details of your subject.

10. Play in a mudhole with a group of toddlers. Watch them as they let the earth ooze through their fingers. Let them teach you the freedom of being intimate with the earth.

Did you know that in the Ojibwe culture the field mouse is the animal symbol of intimacy? In order to survive, the mouse must know its territory well. The mouse builds its nest in underground tunnels or in hollowed logs and tree stumps. It does not travel far from its nest for the berries, fruits, leaves, and seeds it needs for food. It must know where food and water sources can be located under the cover of the grasses. The mouse notices even slight changes in shadow and cloud cover for a change may signal a hawk flying overhead.

Did You Know?

Like a mouse, the naturalist in "Welcome Home" knew her homestead intimately, noticing the changing patterns of wildflowers, birds, and animals. Careful observation over many seasons and years will help you understand your part of the world, whether it is a tiny backyard or a great forest.

In their attempts to catch trout, anglers have gained an intimate knowledge of the insect world that makes up the major portion of the diet of most species of trout. As early as the fifteenth century, Dame Juliana Berners wrote about fishing and the world of insects. Throughout the twentieth century the subject of mayflies and their life cycle has been a focus of anglers and their literature. In 1950, with the publication of *A Modern Dry-Fly Code,* Vincent Marinaro joined many others in encouraging the intentional study of the insect world.

Anglers who fished the Letort river in Western Pennsylvania had for years observed trout swimming near the surface and creating a bulge on top of the water. The conventional wisdom was that they were not feeding but engaging in a peculiar unexplained activity. Marinaro sat and watched. As he was drawn more deeply into the details of the stream, he noted that the trout were indeed feeding on minuscule mayflies, beetles, and ants. Careful observation and intimacy were the gateway to this discovery.

Ecologists look for changes in the ecosystems they study. They observe particular plant or animal species as indicators when they explore new situations or evaluate large areas. Plants are especially useful in analyzing water and soil conditions. Shifts in population densities between animal species in a given area can indicate an imbalanced ecosystem.

Intimate knowledge of ecosystems made observers aware of many current environmental problems. Rachel Carson noted in *Silent Spring* the apparent effects farmland pesticides had on nearby birds, insects, and roadside vegetation. As a trained scientist, she spent four years researching the changes that occurred after the introduction of large-scale pesticide use. With the publication of *Silent Spring*, the environmental movement was born and *ecology* became a household word.

Resources

The Amateur Naturalist's Diary and *The Amateur Naturalist's Handbook* by Vinson Brown. Englewood Cliffs, N.J.: Prentice-Hall, 1983, 1980.

Wit and Wisdom of the Great Outdoors by Jerry Wilber. Duluth, Minn.: Pfeifer-Hamilton Publishers, 1993.

The Curious Naturalist by John Mitchell. Englewood Cliffs, N.J.: Prentice-Hall, 1980.

The Kids' Nature Book: 365 Indoor/Outdoor Activities and Experiences by Susan Milford. Charlotte, Vt.: Williamson Publishing, 1989.

Wandering Through Winter, North with the Spring, Journey into Summer, and *Autumn Across America* by Edwin Way Teale. New York: Dodd, Mead and Company, 1965.

A Modern Dry-Fly Code by Vincent C. Marinaro. New York: Crown Publishers, 1950.

Selective Trout by Doug Swisher and Carl Richards. New York: Crown Publishers, 1971.

The Reasons for Seasons: The Great Cosmic Megagalactic Trip without Moving from Your Chair by Linda Allison. Boston: Little, Brown and Company, 1975.

Trust

To trust someone brings pleasure. It is a joy to live without insecurity, worry, or defensiveness.

Learning to trust another is a gradual process. Trust occurs when enough time has been spent, enough experiences shared, enough investment established to allow a relationship to emerge. When trust develops, the need to control disappears.

The more time you spend with the earth, the more you can trust your experience. The activities and stories in this section are designed to help you learn to trust the earth.

Trust

Learn
to trust
the earth.

Submission

From an early age we are taught to be strong and independent. This strength usually serves us well, but sometimes we need to submit to strength and power outside ourselves.

Recognizing the power of the earth is an important part of being human. Submitting to that power is an act of trust.

The wind is a powerful force. The boys in "Against the Wind" experience its power and submit. They learn that submission is not surrender. It is an opportunity.

Against the Wind

"We'll be back in time for supper and we expect you to be here, too," Alice announced as she and her sister got into the car to drive to town for groceries and a little shopping. "You boys are free as soon as the lunch dishes are done. But remember, if you go out in the dinghy, don't leave the bay."

As she mentioned the bay, Mark, the oldest of her sons, looked out at the glassy surface of the lake. It was unusually flat for this time of day in the middle of June. The local summer weather pattern usually produced brisk winds from nine in the morning until two hours before sundown. But today, just after lunch, the lake was as still as in the evening.

"We're not even going to start the dishes until you get in here, too," his brother John called from the kitchen door. As Mark entered the kitchen, his cousin Tom, the third member of their summer trio, suggested afternoon plans. "Let's take the dinghy out for white bass. With the lake this still they might bite like they do in the evening."

With the plan formulated and the dishes done, they loaded the dinghy, a small flat-bottomed plywood rowboat,

and headed out for silvers, the local term for white bass.

"I sure am glad the wind didn't come up yet," Mark said as they rowed out to their favorite spot in the bay.

When they stopped rowing, John was the first to cast his dollfly, a lead-headed hook covered with yellow bucktail. The ripples from his cast blended with the last of the dinghy's wake. All three settled into the rhythm of cast and retrieve.

After ten minutes, Tom stopped and watched Mark, who was standing in the front of the boat, arch his lure high against the moving clouds.

"The wind is blowing up there like it should be at this time of day," Tom thought as he marveled at the difference between the still surface air and the rapid movement of the clouds from the northwest to the southeast.

"Nothing's biting," John said as he put down his rod and leaned back against the gunwale of the boat.

Mark concurred, "I guess the fish aren't fooled by this still weather. Silvers only bite at dusk and dawn in this lake. We may just as well go home and stop wasting our time."

"Let's row out to Hermit's Island," Tom suggested. "The water's so calm, I'll bet we can row the half-mile out there in twenty minutes or less."

Action was their only reply. Mark and John each took an oar and turned the dinghy toward the island. "Let's see if we can find the hermit's cabin," Mark said.

The boat glided over the flat water with great speed. Within fifteen minutes Mark spotted a wall of weeds just under the surface of the water. "I heard that this whole bay is full of weeds," he said.

"And full of largemouth bass, too," John said as he stopped rowing and cast towards the island.

"Don't waste your time," Tom said. "You'll get nothing but weeds."

John didn't say anything as he pulled twelve inches of hornwort from the end of his line and then wiped his hands on his jeans. With Mark rowing, they landed the boat on a boulder beach and climbed out to continue their exploration.

"Let's find the hermit's cabin," John said. "Someone said that he had an airstrip here."

"If he was a hermit, why would he have an airstrip?" Tom countered. "Who would he be flying to see? I don't even think there ever was a hermit here. It's just rumor. Let's hike out to the north end of the island."

As they approached the point of the island, they heard a familiar sound. The crashing of waves. "The wind is up," Mark noted. "We had better head home."

"We'll never make it against this wind," Tom said. "It will be directly in our faces. I think we should wait until it dies down."

"Do you want to be the one to tell our moms we left the bay?" Mark asked in a way that needed no answer. "One of us can sit in the front of the dinghy to hold the bow down while the other two row."

They ran back to the dinghy, beached on the protected south shore of the island. The treetops bent in the wind, pointing out their predicament. Mark and Tom each grabbed an oar as John took the first shift in the bow of the boat. The waves were getting higher on the leeward side of the island. John worried about what would happen as they rounded the corner into the wind. "Maybe we should wait a bit," he said, supporting Tom's words of caution. "I'd rather be in a little trouble than sink the dinghy. Then we'd be in big trouble."

"We're in no trouble at all," Mark responded. "We'll pull hard and steady. I'm not changing my plans for a little wind."

A wall of wind and whitecaps waited for them. The dinghy climbed to the top of each wave and seemed to hold there in midair, waiting for the great wind to drive them back. Mark and Tom pulled against the wind together, first leaning forward and then straining backward with their legs and backs. The dinghy hung suspended, making no forward progress. It took all of their strength just to avoid being blown beyond the island into the large lake basin.

"Let's go back in," John shouted above the wind. "If we keep rowing we'll swing out from the island and blow fifteen miles across the lake, if we live that long."

"I agree," Tom said as he stopped rowing in exhaustion. The boat swung around and started to blow back toward the point and the shelter of the island. "I'm tired. You're tired. And this is dangerous. Sometimes a person has to give up."

Mark grabbed both oars and pulled against the wind. "I don't need any more trouble from Mom. We better be home when they get there. If they find out that we took the dinghy out here, we'll never use it again."

He pulled desperately as the boat started sliding back towards the point. John watched their course closely, worrying they would drift out beyond the reach of the island shelter.

"Give it up, Mark," Tom pleaded. "No trouble with our moms is worth this. Let's rest on the island and go home when we can. The wind has got to stop sometime."

Mark shook his head and kept on rowing. It seemed wrong to quit. The rhythm of the wind and waves had a hold on him. He would not, could not, surrender.

And then, he did. He stopped rowing. The battle was over. The dinghy drifted silently with the wind. After a moment, Tom grabbed the oars and steered them around the point and into shelter.

This was right. Mark now knew it. The others had known it earlier. They would wait for the wind to die down.

Submit to the Earth

Purpose: To recognize the earth's power, the limitations it places on humans, and appropriate times to submit.

Participants: While this activity is largely for individuals, a parent or friend can lead a child by example. For reasons of safety, some aspects of this activity are recommended only for children ages twelve and up.

Setting: Outdoors by a lake, a river, the sea, or a prairie.

Materials: A force or cycle in nature—the wind, the sun, the sea.

How-To: The first step in recognizing the power of nature is to immerse yourself in it. Use all your senses to explore it. On a windy day, stretch your arms out to embrace the wind. Let your clothes flutter in its wake. While paddling a canoe or rowing a boat, set aside your paddle or oar and let the boat drift with the current or waves. While outside on a sunny day, feel the intensity of the sun on your body by standing still for a few minutes.

Try to continue the activity with which you were engaged. Walk against a strong wind. Paddle against the current. Work vigorously outside despite the heat. Continue doing the activity until exhaustion sets in. With safety in mind, go to the edge of your abilities. Remember, the point of this activity is to recognize the power of the earth, not to compete with it. Caution must be taken at each step of this activity.

Recognizing the limitations of your skill or endurance, let go again. Seek shelter.

Other Ideas for Submitting to the Earth

1. On a windy March day, go outside to fly a kite. Release a large amount of string and watch the flight. Increase tension on the string. Play with the wind by resisting and submitting to it. Which works best for flying a kite?

2. The next time you're on a lake in a sailboat, sail to each point of the compass, each point of the wind. Which point of sail

provides the most speed and efficiency? Is the fastest point of sail one of resistance or submission?

3. When planning a vacation, do you account for the weather? On any outing, whether an afternoon picnic, a weekend at a cabin or resort, or a trip into the mountains, be aware of weather conditions and be prepared to cancel or change plans.

4. For a family or school activity, play this game of limited resources. Decide as a group how much food or gasoline you use on the average per week. Set aside the amount of money it will take to purchase these resources and spend no more. At the end of the week, discuss what living with limited resources means.

5. While on a river, paddle downstream with the current. Bring the boat to the riverbank, turn around and try to paddle upstream.

6. Find a grassy hill. Try to roll a marble uphill to the top, at least for twenty or thirty yards. Now roll the marble downhill. Set up teams with friends. Don't carry the marble, keep it in contact with the ground.

7. Gather a large number of friends or schoolmates. Divide the group into teams and play tug-of-war in a variety of areas—flat and hilly. How much difference does the terrain make? Do those who are pulling uphill always lose?

Did you know that hawks ride the winds in order to travel thousands of miles? Their survival, like that of Mark, Tom, and John in "Against the Wind," depends on their willingness to submit to the winds rather than fight them.

As hawks begin their spring and fall migrations, they gather at the base of a mountain or steep hill and wait for the formation of updrafts. (Updrafts are created when prevailing winds blow against the slope.) Perhaps hawks' most dramatic use of the wind takes place when hundreds of them use thermals. (Thermals are columns of warm air rising from the ground.) Hawks spiral upward in the thermal, rising to thousands of feet above the earth. When the thermal dissipates, the hawks soar over the terrain for up to two miles. They can travel at speeds of forty miles per hour in this manner.

Migration is the natural response of a number of species of fish, birds, mammals, and insects to the changing demands of spring and fall. This movement, which helps to ensure the survival of a species, is a surrender to the realities of the environment.

Survival, in community and on the earth, requires an understanding of our own limitations and the environment's. Humans must recognize when submission is an appropriate response for survival of their species and the earth itself.

In the 1930s, the rich farmlands of the Midwest were nearly destroyed by a series of destructive wind and dust storms. To grow more food, farmers had cleared away trees to create large, open fields. They overgrazed grasslands and employed intensive farming techniques. These farming practices combined with a natural drought cycle to produce dust bowls. Fifty million acres of land were damaged during the decade, and an additional fifty million acres were endangered before conservation measures were adopted. In the middle of this crisis, the Soil Conservation Service was established to teach farmers ways to slow soil erosion, to submit to the natural contours of land, and to anticipate the water cycles of nature while still producing food.

Recognizing the need to understand and submit to the earth's cycles and to its limited resources opens our eyes to other opportunities. Dealing with the finite nature of oil, coal, and gas reserves provides an opportunity for exploration of solar, wind, and geothermal energy production. Looking at patterns of land use for the production of food, particularly livestock, allows food specialists to present alternatives to the meat-heavy diet of most Americans.

Submitting to the reality of limited resources and adapting to natural cycles of the earth ensures the survival of individuals and communities.

Resources

Peter Kagan and the Wind by Gordon Bok. Sharon, Conn.: Folk Legacy Records, Inc.

The Fall of Freddie the Leaf by Leo Buscaglia. Thorofare, N.J.: Charles B. Slack, 1982.

Limits to Growth by Dennis Meadows. New York: Potomac Associates, 1972.

High in the Wind: The Snow Geese by Lynn M. Stone. Vero Beach, Fla: The Rourke Corporation, 1991.

Trust

Learn
to trust
the earth.

Security

Security, sought by many living things, carries with it the freedom to grow and flourish. There is security in being in the right place at the right time. Being with the earth is often being in that right place.

We have come from the earth. Touching the earth will restore a sense of security. First, there may be fear, but given time, the earth can calm those fears.

In the following story, Grandma Essie learns, with the help of her family and the passage of time, to feel secure in the woods.

Something for Everyone

When Marty came in the back door, she was met by her six-year-old daughter, Sarah.

"Mom, hurry. There's a great big letter from Grandma on the table." Sarah ran from the door to the kitchen table, grabbed a manila envelope, and met her mother before she was three steps into the kitchen. "Open it up. It's addressed to you but look what she wrote on the back."

Marty took the envelope, turned it over, and saw in her mother's handwriting, "Something for everyone."

"Open it up," Sarah demanded with excitement. Mail was always special to Sarah, especially mail from her grandmother.

Marty opened the metal clasp, lifted the flap, and withdrew a stack of papers. She read aloud from the first page.

My Dear Family,

I have now been back in my St. Paul apartment for one week since spending the last month with you at Partridge Point. I feel better right now than I have since since Grandpa Tom died. Your invitation for me to join you on your summer vacation was just what I needed. I have been thinking about the last month since I returned home and decided to *write each one of you a letter with my thoughts. Read on.*

Love,

Grandma Essie

"Where's mine?" Sarah asked as she started to reach for the pile.

Marty sorted through the pile and handed her a single sheet addressed "Dear Sarah."

Sarah took her letter, looked it over and handed it back to her mother. "Would you read it to me, Mom? It's regular writing, not printing. I can't read it."

Marty took the letter and began to read aloud.

Dear Sarah,

I hope that you are enjoying your last month of summer vacation. I certainly enjoyed my month with you.

Last night as I went to sleep I listened to the sound of my air conditioner in the window and thought of sharing the room with you at the cabin. I remembered the first night when we went to bed. I kept closing the window and you kept opening it. Finally I said, "Sarah, we must leave this window shut. It's just too noisy to sleep with it open." Your response was simple. You said, "That's not noise, Grandma. That's just frogs and crickets." Believe it or not, Sarah, last night I missed those frogs and crickets. They make a peaceful sound to sleep by. I miss you, too.

One of our best times together was the morning walk to the bay. We checked on the two duck families who spent the nights in that protected water. Some days I didn't really want to go. I think you knew that. Yet we both enjoyed watching the ducks swim away from us into open water for their daily outing. The mother ducks would swim first, quacking a warning to us, with a trail of little ones behind. Each day we would count the ducklings to make sure that they all had made it through the night safely.

Thank you, Sarah, for being my roommate and for sharing your joy in that special place in the woods.

Love, Grandma Essie

When Marty finished, she gathered up the letters and said, "Let's have everyone read their letter at the supper table. It will be like having Grandma here for supper." She put the letters away and prepared supper.

As soon as they finished eating, Joshua, the first born and first done with dinner, picked up his plate and excused himself. "Wait a minute," his mother said.

"We have something special tonight." She went over to the cupboard and got the letters. "I have a letter for each of you from Grandma. I thought it would be fun to read them first and then give every one a chance to share them aloud if they want." She distributed the letters to her husband and each of the children.

Joshua spoke first. "I'll read mine aloud first, and then I have to get over to school for practice."

He read:

Dear Joshua,

I think that you are the one to thank for my being able to stay at Partridge Point for the entire month. I remember the night when I drove down that long road to the Point. I felt awful. I know now that it was fear. The beauty of the woods that your dad is always talking about seemed dangerous to me. As I pulled up in my car and saw you and your brother Soren sitting on the bridge waiting for me, I thought to myself, "I'll stay for the weekend and then go home." You made the difference for me. How? It might sound silly, but you were willing to go to town with me every day. I don't know if it was that new driver's permit you had or just the chance to see people your own age in town, but whenever I wanted to go to town, you were ready to come along. Everyone else laughed and teased me about my shopping addiction. You came along.

Thank you. Because you helped me touch base with a world that was familiar to me, I also learned to be comfortable in one that wasn't.

Keep driving safely,

Grandma Essie

Soren started to read his letter aloud before anyone could say a word.

Dear Soren,

I do believe that you belong in the woods. I was constantly amazed at how you could spend time by the lake, back by the bog, or on the trail without being bored.

I remember standing in the kitchen and watching you sit alone on the dock in the back bay one evening. I noticed you there when I started the dishes. You were still there when they were all done. I pointed this out to your dad and asked him what you were doing out there for so long.

"Nothing," he said. "He's just enjoying himself. Why don't you join him?"

So I did. Remember? I came and sat by you for a long time. We talked a little bit but mostly we just sat, listened, and looked. You pointed out a school of minnows that kept hovering near the dock. Shiners, you called them. I think that those moments with you were the first time that I was really comfortable in the woods. It was so quiet and so beautiful.

For eleven years old, I think you have taught your grandmother quite a bit.

Thank you and keep it up,

Grandma Essie

"I really need to go to school," Joshua said as he grabbed his gym bag. "Mom and Dad, you can fill me in on your letters later. Is that okay?"

Marty answered him. "I'll save them for you. You can read them yourself. Don't be late."

As Joshua went out the front door, his dad began to read his letter.

Dear Griff,

Not every son-in-law would have welcomed his mother-in-law along on his annual vacation the way you welcomed me. You not only welcomed me but encouraged me to come.

I remember you telling me at Christmas that I needed the peace of the Point. I must admit that you were right.

As the weeks went by, I became more and more comfortable there. The rhythms of the place calmed me and made me feel secure. The sight of the setting sun against Pelican Island in the distance. The songs of birds in the morning and the chirps of crickets at night. The distant sounds of outboard motors, of waves lapping the shoreline, of loons laughing in the evening. The sound of human laughter was important, too. I remember you and me laughing each evening as the fellow in the red boat would come by at exactly the same time. He sat up in that boat like he was leading the navy on an important detail. You used to say, "Walleyes, beware. The commodore is after you now."

Thank you, Griff, for sharing Partridge Point with me. Thank you for your patience with my fear. I'm a little embarrassed at how I checked the doors three or four times before going to bed during my first weeks there. And I kept locking them in the daytime, although no one came down the path for the entire month we were there. I guess I needed time to get used to the silence. And the seclusion. It frightened me. Then it gave me peace. Thanks.

Love,

Essie

Griff set his letter in front of him at the table and said quietly, "One more to go. Let's hear what Grandma wrote to her daughter."

Marty smiled at her family and said, "The last few minutes have been worth a lot to me. There were moments last month when I worried that having my mother along would spoil the month for everyone. She was so uncomfortable and

nervous about being there. She acted like it was the north pole or something. I guess the nervousness was just a sign that she needed this vacation." Then Marty read her letter:

Dear Marty,

I've always enjoyed your family, and we have been lucky to live close enough to each other to share many holidays and birthdays. Yet it took this last month for me to realize how much I enjoy living with others. I hadn't been that happy since I was much younger.

I don't believe it was just the family that was responsible for the happiness. I think that the setting contributed: rocks, trees, the smell of the lake, and the promise of fish suppers. Each day was part of a gentle summer rhythm, from walking with Sarah to talking with you and Griff. The summer heat and the occasional storm all were like punctuation to lives lived well. I felt like I belonged there. And you know what? Now that I'm home again, I even feel more like I belong here.

Health. You, your family, and the earth gave my health back this summer. And I love you all for it.

Mom

Marty gathered everyone's letters and put them back in the envelope. "Let's save these letters," she said. "We all might need to hear them again in the middle of next winter. I think that Grandma Essie has done a good job of telling our stories about the Point. In fact, she may have taught us a thing or two."

Feel Secure with the Earth

Purpose: To take a two- to four-week vacation with the earth and become secure in an outdoor setting.

Participants: Families of all ages and sizes.

Setting: A resort or a national or state park or forest.

Materials: Brochures from local chambers of commerce, resort associations, or national and state parks and forests; camping equipment (tent, sleeping bags, cooking equipment) and food if you are establishing a campsite; food and bedding if you are staying at a resort; all-weather clothing; recreational equipment for exploring.

How-To: Decide to spend this year's family vacation in one spot. Pick a place on the earth you would like to visit for two to four weeks. Contact chambers of commerce, state conservation departments, or the national park or forest district within your state for information about places to stay. Resorts, established campgrounds, or backcountry camping sites are a few of the possibilities.

Read about the natural features of the area prior to your vacation: the flora and fauna that inhabit the area, interesting geological formations, and recreational opportunities (fishing, hiking, boating, berry-picking). Select the equipment you will need to explore this area.

Upon arriving at your destination, set up your new homestead. You will be calling this cabin or campsite home for the next few weeks. Make yourself comfortable: establish kitchen, sleeping, and living room quarters.

Be sensitive to the rising and setting of the sun. Set your internal clocks to the earth's clock. Look for animal patterns that reflect a rhythm of sunup and sundown. Watch for people patterns, too.

Relax. Establish a rhythm of rest, exploration, activity, relaxation, and reflection. Note what makes each member of your family comfortable or uneasy in this home in the woods or lakeshore. Help each other adapt, just as you would help each other move into a new house or apartment.

You can trust the natural world if you know what to expect: study weather patterns and guess what may be coming the next day; observe the movements and calls of animals and birds—when they can be seen and what they do; discover changes in the plant community as flowers become fruit and buds become leaves; recognize other cycles and patterns of the earth.

When you return home, use a trip letter or journal entries to share with friends or family members your discovery that you belong outdoors with the earth.

1. Take a vacation to the same cabin, resort, or park over a period of years.

2. Get up with the sun, go to bed when it's dark. Don't use any artificial lights all day. Seek places where light occurs naturally.

3. Pick a favorite plant or animal. Read about its life cycle or

Other Ideas for Feeling Secure with the Earth

watch it over a year. Diagram its life cycle—from seed to flower to fruit, from birth to mating to death.

4. Discover your own hunger cycle. Instead of eating at a specific time, eat when you're hungry. Note the pattern over a period of a couple days. When on vacation, notice changes that occur in your diet. Do you eat different things at different times? Why?

5. Watch for phenomena that recur in the world that surrounds you: hatches of insects; feeding patterns for birds, squirrels, deer, and fish; emergence of floral life in wetlands; appearance of berries.

6. Introduce toddlers to camping at an early age. Begin with camping out in your backyard, then overnight at a local park. Help them notice the details and the differences from home.

7. Keep a family vacation journal. Have every member of the family contribute their observations. Store the journal with any photographs taken during the trip.

8. Get to know one state or national park very well. Choose one that is close enough that you can visit it regularly and attempt to experience it in a variety of ways: through using interpretation aids, hiking and camping, reading stories and legends about the area, learning its history, and getting near the park's boundaries and edges rather than its highpoints and main attractions.

9. On the first night of a camping trip, talk about any fears you may have. Find out ways to overcome those fears during the course of your camping trip.

Did you know that it takes time to feel secure with the earth? For Grandma Essie, it took a month's vacation in lake country. Nature was frightening to her at first, but eventually she learned to trust the new sights and sounds. The power of nature might be frightening when you first begin to explore the earth.

Aboriginal peoples developed a sense of security with the earth. They spent each day of their lives living with the earth, depending on it for food and shelter. They observed patterns in the weather and in the activities of animals, and seasonal transitions in the plant world. The Ojibwe people of northern Wisconsin and Minnesota found security in the rhythms of the earth's seasons, moving throughout the forest as resources became available: to wooded areas for late winter maple syruping, to spring sites near inland lake fishing, to summer villages near good hunting grounds, and to fall sites where wild rice, berries, and nuts could be gathered in preparation for winter.

As small towns grew into large cities, the earth became less a home and more a place to visit. But the need to connect with the earth and feel the security of its rhythms remained. Summer resorts and retreats drew the wealthy away from city living. Unusual natural areas became spots to develop summer homes.

The Apostle Islands, a twenty-two island archipelago off the coast of northern Wisconsin in Lake Superior, became a mecca for people from St. Louis, Omaha, Chicago, and Minneapolis-St. Paul. Cottages were built at the turn of the century on the main island, Madeline. A number of other summer homesteads were built on the surrounding islands. The water and the isolation of island living were the attractions. The summer residents spent three months of every year touching the earth and calling Madeline Island their home.

Did You Know?

67

In 1970 the National Park Service recognized the natural beauty of this area and established Apostle Islands National Lakeshore. Although summer residents still return to Madeline Island, summer cottages and second homes on the other islands have been replaced with campsites and hiking trails open to the public. The beauty of the islands, which drew summer residents one hundred years ago, now draws backpackers, sea kayakers, and sailboaters. Visitors can spend a day, a weekend, or up to two weeks at campsites.

The National Park Service was established in 1872 to preserve natural wonders, historic places, and outdoor recreation sites for the benefit and enjoyment of the people. Yellowstone was the first park established. Today, more than 330 natural sites, totaling over 124,000 square miles, exist. Every state except Delaware has at least one national park. The parks are preserved for their outstanding beauty or scientific importance. To that end, the parklands are kept in their unspoiled condition. Plants and animals are left as undisturbed as possible. Parks truly are places to experience nature and develop a security with the land on which you camp or recreate. In many of the national parks, you can camp at a particular site for two weeks.

The National Forest Service was established in 1891. National forests are managed for multiple use wood products, grazing, water development, mining, and recreation. The 155 national forests in the United States and Puerto Rico have a large variety of habitats: deserts; rain forests; mountains; grasslands; glacial and inland lakes; and pine, hemlock, and hardwood forests. Nine states have no national forests: Massachusetts, Connecticut, North Dakota, Rhode Island, New Jersey, Kansas, Hawaii, Delaware, and Iowa. In the national forests, visitors camp, picnic, hunt, fish, boat, canoe, swim, horseback ride, and participate in winter sports. In the national forests, just as in national parks, people can spend two weeks at a particular campsite. Each national forest has a specific management plan and fee structure for camping which can be obtained by contacting the forest supervisor.

Explore the national parks and forests near your home and in other areas of the country. In their unspoiled beauty you can develop a secure relationship with the earth.

Resources

The Complete Guide to America's National Parks. New York: The National Park Foundation, Prentice-Hall Travel, 1992.

The Field Guide to U.S. National Forests: Region by Region, State by State by Robert H. Mohlenbrock. New York: Congdon and Weed, 1984.

Off the Beaten Path: A Guide to More than 1000 Scenic and Interesting Places Still Uncrowded and Inviting edited by Carroll C. Calkins. Pleasantville, N.Y.: The Reader's Digest Association, 1987.

Why Do the Seasons Change: Questions on Nature's Rhythms and Cycles by Dr. Philip Whitfield and Joyce Pope. New York: Viking Penguin, 1987.

Gift from the Sea by Anne Morrow Lindbergh. New York: Vintages Books, 1978.

A Place in the Woods by Helen Hoover. New York: Alfred A. Knopf, 1966.

Trust

Learn
to trust
the earth.

Commitment

"I will." Words of commitment. These words are heard at important human events such as weddings and inaugurations and at many other times when people make promises.

Commitment is instinctual throughout the world of nature. Wolves mate for life. Birds raise helpless nestlings. Commitment for them is a way of life.

Follow the Mercek family as they decide to build and maintain a bluebird trail. Then, make your own commitment to the earth.

On the Trail

On a snowy Saturday morning in January, the Mercek family began an adventure that would fill their summers for years to come. While having morning coffee with Milt, their neighbor, the whole family was invited downstairs to view his winter project, building twenty-five new houses for his bluebird trail. The basement was filled with scrap wood and new cedar.

"This is my cure for the winter blues," Milt said as he picked up an assembled bluebird house. "I feel much closer to spring when I get to this stage of building. These are Sand Hill boxes. I also have some interesting angled houses called Peterson boxes, designed by a Minnesotan. I'll bet you can guess his name: Peterson. Richard Peterson."

He grabbed a piece of wood from a stack of parts waiting for assembly. "Building and designing houses is a good way of making a bluebird trail a year-long activity," Milt said, examining a piece of wood.

"I'd like to keep a trail, too!" Linda, the youngest of the Merceks, exclaimed.

"I think that would be too large a commitment for someone your age, Linda," her mother warned. "They need regular care. Don't they, Milt?"

"They do need to be checked regularly throughout the summer," Milt responded. "I have a suggestion." He walked over to the pile of new cedar boards. "Why don't the four of you come back after lunch and we'll build four houses from this wood, one for each member of your family. When spring comes you can create the Mercek family bluebird trail at the end of mine."

"How can just four houses be a trail?" Linda asked.

"Bluebird trails can range from two houses to the longest trail, which runs five hundred miles from North Battlefield, Saskatchewan to Macgregor, Manitoba. That trail is made up of many smaller trails."

Linda's father, Dean, was interested, yet cautious. "What kind of commitment would we be making?"

"I think a short weekly walk through the woods in the summer would be perfect," Milt responded. "Some people get by with as few as seven visits a season."

"How exciting can looking at a bunch of birdhouses be?" twelve-year-old Vince asked as he created an airplane with two pieces of scrap wood.

"There is much more to maintaining a bluebird trail than just looking at the houses, Vince," Milt responded. He looked at each member of the family and focused on Dean. "How about it? The houses are easy to build. The birds aren't fussy. Do we build this afternoon?"

The afternoon was spent measuring, sawing, and nailing.

Two months later, while the last of the March snow still lay in dirty piles, they loaded the trunk of Milt's car with their four houses. "I put up twenty-five houses last week," Milt told them with pride. "I kept an eye out for places for your houses."

They stopped at a cemetery five miles out of town. "Cemeteries, meadows, and golf courses are all good places for a trail," Milt said as they unloaded the houses. "It's important to keep the houses out of the deep woods, but close to a grove of trees. The adults won't nest in the woods, but the young fledglings need cover nearby when they are learning to fly."

Linda ran to the base of a tree. "Let's put one on this tree, Milt," she said as she tapped the trunk of a large oak tree.

"They won't nest there, Linda," he said shaking his head. "That tree is alive. Bluebirds nest in dead trees. That's why the population decreased so much. People no longer use wooden fenceposts, and they work hard to keep dead trees off their property. Natural spots for bluebirds to nest are more rare than they used to be."

"Now I understand why we brought these two-by-fours," Dean said. "We'll make our own fenceposts."

Milt showed Dean where to put the two-by-fours. "This should be a perfect spot for the first house," he noted. "We'll stretch your trail out starting here and heading west, placing the houses about fifteen hundred feet apart. That may seem like a long distance, but bluebirds are territorial. They would fight with each other if we placed the houses any closer together.

"Different species of birds, however, are willing to share territory. One of the other birds that use this size house is the tree swallow. Some bluebird trails have become tree swallow trails."

"What's wrong with that?" Linda asked.

"Nothing, but they don't need our help as much as bluebirds do," Milt added. "Some people set their houses out in pairs so that the tree swallows can have one house while the bluebirds take the other. Neither species will nest close to another of the same species, but the two will nest near each other. Companion houses provide space for everyone."

"How is the bluebird population doing now?" Dean asked as they walked along the woods.

"Since the restoration movement began, the population is really coming back," Milt answered. "I don't know any statistics, but I see almost fifty times as many bluebirds as I saw twenty years ago." He pounded down the two-by-four. "We are making some progress. I'm certain of that."

Three weeks later, the Merceks returned to check their trail. Linda led the group as she ran up to the first bird house. "Can I look first?" she asked as she lifted the lid of the box. She jumped back with a little scream. "There's something in there."

"That's the purpose of these houses, Linda," Milt laughed. "Let's see who has nested here." He lifted the lid and reached inside the box. He came out with a handful of stick, straw, feathers, and string. "English sparrows," he grunted with disgust as he shredded the nest and tossed it away. "They not only don't need our help, they would completely take over the trail if we let them. They were imported into our country and now they multiply like weeds. Weeds of the bird world, that's what they are," he said shaking his head.

Linda raced to reach the next house. This time she was ready for anything. "There are eggs in this one," she exclaimed. "Are they bluebird eggs?"

Milt looked. "This is a tree swallow nest. You can tell by the white feathers woven into the nest. Let's leave this one alone."

The third house was empty, but the fourth house had something waiting for them. A nest, made mostly from pine needles, was topped neatly with three light-blue eggs. "Here it is, Linda," Milt said. "Your first bluebird nest. Let's head back to the car and write down our findings."

Dean was assigned to keep the records for their trail, so he noted the results of the day's tour in the trail notebook. He planned to send a monthly report to the state Audubon Society.

"I'm so glad we have some bluebirds," Linda said. "Let's build more boxes."

Her mother laughed and said, "I think four is enough for this year, Linda. But I suspect that our trail will grow over the years."

Make a Commitment to the Earth

Purpose: To make a commitment to the earth by creating and maintaining a bluebird trail for one year.

Participants: Work in family units or in groups of three to five people, with at least one adult involved.

Setting: Trails can be established on the edge of town near a wooded area, or along the edges of open areas such as golf courses and cemeteries, but not in deep woods.

Materials: An approved bluebird house design, wood, hammer, saw, tape measure, nails, and notebook.

How-To: Consult a field guide to determine if bluebirds nest in your area. Obtain a bluebird house design from the North American Bluebird Association, Box 6295, Silver Springs, Maryland.

Several house designs are available: Peterson, Olson, Hill Lake, and Companion. Common features include an entrance of one to one-and-a half inches without a perch, a box at least six inches deep made out of rough wood, a roof that can be opened for cleaning and inspection, and ventilation holes.

Set the boxes outside. They need to be three to five feet off the ground on a wooden fencepost or utility pole. Always check with the landowner before placing a box on private property. Face the boxes twenty-five to one hundred feet from shrubbery or a wooded area, placing them at least fifteen hundred feet apart.

When spring arrives, begin a weekly tour of the bluebird trail. At first, bluebirds may not discover their new rent-free housing. Be patient, they will. Check for nests of competing species such as English sparrows and tree swallows. Many bluebirders remove the nests of English sparrows, knowing they will find other places to nest. Check for infestations of insects such as blowworms and ants, thoroughly cleaning the nesting box if you find any. Most important, look for bluebird eggs. In your trail notebook, record whatever you find, noting the date, the location, and other information such as the number of eggs.

Check with the state conservation department or the North American Bluebird Association for the address of a local group or person who collects this data. By sending your data to them, you will likely be rewarded with further information about others maintaining trails and the knowledge that you are a part of a team effort to restore the bluebird population.

Other Ideas for Making a Commitment to the Earth

1. Set up a bird feeder. When this is done in the fall, it needs to be continued throughout the winter.

2. Join a group dedicated to the conservation of a particular species. Trout Unlimited, Loon Watch, Timber Wolf Alliance, and The Whale Foundation are possibilities.

3. Become familiar with a local nature center. Commit yourself as a family or group of friends to attend two or three programs a year. It's a great way to get to know the earth.

4. Humans require many resources just to live: air, water, food, shelter, and energy, for example. Select one of these resources and commit yourself to improving your relationship with the earth by using that resource more carefully.

5. Take charge of your family's garbage for one week. Analyze it for things that can be composted, recycled, and reused. Weigh each pile of garbage, and then set a goal for waste reduction. Continue the process of weighing the separated trash for a month as family members take week-long turns competing to see who can eliminate the most waste.

6. Develop or join an effort to regularly pick up litter along a mile-long stretch of highway.

7. Teach your preschooler to take care of your house plants. Show the child how to water and fertilize them, and how to trim off dead leaves.

8. If you have a pet dog, cat, gerbil, bird, or hamster, turn over their care to your children for a week. Make a list of responsibilities and record their completion.

9. Create a flower garden for your church, neighborhood, or city park and maintain it for a season.

Did you know that only a few inches below the surface of the ground, you'll find extensive trail systems? These trails provide home and safe nesting places for ants.

As a family, the Merceks created a trail of bluebird houses and committed themselves to its upkeep. Working together they were more effective than if they worked separately—and they also had more fun.

Ants are social beings, too. They live together in colonies to better accomplish all the work. A queen ant rules over hundreds of male ants and thousands of worker ants. You can find ants by looking under rocks and large stones or by searching for an anthill. The worker ants build an anthill by bringing the dirt from excavating their tunnels and nesting chambers to the surface. If an ant home is disturbed by human activity or rainstorm, the worker ants quickly muster forces to repair damage, rebuild passageways, and move eggs and larvae to new chambers.

The beaver, known to Native Americans as "the little brother of men," also lives in colonies. Beavers, the largest rodents in the north woods, are known for their resourcefulness and ability to alter their environment, a quality shared with humans.

When a beaver leaves its parent's home, it seeks to establish its own territory. The beaver begins this process either by finding a small stream to dam or by burrowing into a riverbank or lakeshore. Beavers begin damming a stream by laying large sticks across a shallow place. Using their head and front legs, they pack stones and mud around the sticks. Beaver dams usually stand three to four feet high and are fifty to two hundred feet across. If any damage occurs to the dam, the beavers hurry to repair it. They work during the night, hauling large sticks and sections of trees they have felled to the water's edge and floating them into place. They wedge in small branches and spread mud with thrusting movements of their paws.

Like their "little brother" the beaver, humans have begun to take a closer look at their environment and have started to repair problems in a more timely fashion. But the territory of humans goes far beyond the few inches of ground an ant colony inhabits or the few acres of water and land a beaver calls home. Over 5.4 billion people live on the earth in all kinds of habitats. Together we are depleting the earth's resources at an alarming rate.

In 1972, the United Nations gathered world leaders in Stockholm, Sweden, for a conference on the environment. Delegates recognized the impact humans made on the earth and saw the need for making a commitment to its preservation. Out of that gathering, the United Nations Environment Programme was established and an action plan of 109 recommendations was developed. International treaties to curb ocean dumping and protect a number of species were signed.

A similar conference was held in 1992 in Rio de Janeiro, Brazil. Over 140 countries sent delegates to this event to listen to reports on the status of the earth. Lester Brown, founder of Worldwatch Institute, commented that the health of the planet had deteriorated dangerously since the Stockholm conference.

Again treaties were signed and recommendations were developed. But recognition and recommendations will not provide care for the earth. The development of possible solutions and implementation plans, along with committed nations and individuals, will. The timeworn adage "Think globally, act locally" is a truth we need to embrace.

Resources

50 Simple Things Kids Can Do to Save the Earth by John Javna and The EarthWorks Group. Kansas City, Mo.: Andrews and McMeel, 1990.

Earth Book for Kids: Activities to Help Heal the Environment by Linda Schwartz. Santa Barbara, Calif.: The Learning Works, 1990.

Keepers of the Earth: Native American Stories and Environmental Activities for Children by Michael J. Caduto and Joseph Bruchac. Golden, Colo.: Fulcrum, 1988.

Keepers of the Animals: Native American Stories and Wildlife Activities for Children by Michael J. Caduto and Joseph Bruchac. Golden, Colo.: Fulcrum, 1991.

For the Birds by Laura Erickson. Illustrations by Jeff Sonstegard. Duluth, Minn.: Pfeifer-Hamilton, 1993.

Nurture

From birth to maturity, people are nurtured. From childhood to old age, people give care. Caring for another is an important aspect of every relationship.

Nurturing occurs as we live in love with someone. Nurturing is the ability to touch and care for another. It is offered in many ways: a soft, gentle caress, the strong hand of discipline, the sage guiding of experience, and the freedom of flight.

Our relationship with the earth is no different than other relationships. Nurturing is an important element. The earth nurtures humans by providing all that they need to live. A good response is to return the nurturing.

In this section, we examine the crises of the earth and its long-term needs as opportunities for nurturing.

As you live in love with the earth, remember to nurture it.

Nurture

Remember
to nurture
the earth.

Response

A mother does not need to be taught to respond to the cries of her child. A cry of pain elicits concern, a shout of joy creates pleasure, an expression of need generates action. Response is a natural outgrowth of relationship.

We hear many calls for response to the environmental crisis. Often, those calls are based only on reason or perhaps on fear. But, we can also respond to the earth's needs with love, respect, and passion.

Read in "The Cry of the Sea" of a boy's love for whales. Then join Eric—respond to the cries of the earth.

The Cry of the Sea

Eric heard a knock on his bedroom door.

"Fifteen minutes to get up, Eric," his mother called.

Eric rolled over, looked out the window, and squinted at the sun rising over the next apartment building. He followed the stream of sunlight as it entered his room. Tiny dust particles illuminated by the light formed an elevated pathway from the window to his white dresser. He imagined being small enough to walk that path.

"Time to get up, little fish," he whispered. Eric put his legs over the edge of the bed, found his slippers, and then shuffled over to his aquarium. Tiny red swordtails, barely an inch long, darted in and out of the sunken ship. The morning sun quickly picked up their iridescent color. Eric's eyes scouted along the gravel for his bottom-feeders. He had learned that both the plants and these bottom feeders helped to clean the tank and keep the fish alive.

"They all work together to make it a healthy and happy world," his mother had explained when they were setting up the tank.

Eric knelt down and pressed his forehead to the glass. He watched how light reflected off the top of the tank. Then he squinted his eyes and looked through the tank. On the wall behind his aquarium he had placed an underwater picture of a humpback whale. When he spotted the picture in a discarded *National Geographic*, he knew that it had to become a part of his underwater world.

Looking at the whale was a way for him to remember last summer's trip to Alaska. He and his family had ridden on the Alaska state ferry system all the way from Seattle, Washington, to Skagway, Alaska. The trip took three days and nights. Eric spent many hours at the rail of the boat watching for porpoises and whales. Once a humpback whale had followed alongside for over an hour. Sometimes she would disappear and Eric would scan the water, waiting for the whale's blustery return to the surface. The whale would swim along and almost talk to Eric.

In that hour a passion was formed. Eric fell in love with that whale, and from that moment, Eric loved all whales. He started collecting pictures and information on many kinds of whales. But his favorite thing to do was to peer through this tank and imagine that he and his whale were in the waters of southeast Alaska.

Eric had even named one of his fish after a famous whale. He had a pale white catfish that he called Moby.

"But where is Moby now?" Eric worried. He looked along the bottom, behind the ship, and around the plants that grew along the sides of his fish tank. "Mom," he cried. "Something's the matter." He ran out of his bedroom and into the kitchen.

"Eric, why aren't you dressed?" she asked. "The school bus will be here in fifteen minutes and you haven't eaten your breakfast."

"Mom, please," Eric said as tears began to form in his eyes. "I can't find Moby."

"He's probably just hiding among the plants," she responded. "We'll look when you get home from school."

"No, Mom, now," Eric tugged at her apron. "I'm afraid that something has happened to him."

Eric raced back to his room, his mother close behind. They both scanned the sides and front of the tank, searching for his treasured fish. "I see him, Mom. Something is wrong."

The catfish wasn't moving as quickly as the other fish were. Its fins were drooping, barely moving at all.

"When is the last time you fed them?" his mother asked.

"Last night before I went to bed," he answered.

"Did you clean out the tank last weekend?" she continued.

"Uh-huh," he responded.

Eric's mother stared at the fish. "It looks like he's having a hard time breathing."

Eric's stomach felt hollow. He glanced at the aerator and realized he hadn't turned it back on after he cleaned the tank on Saturday. While the plants in the tank supplied some oxygen for the fish, it wasn't enough for the number of fish Eric kept. He quickly plugged the aerator back into the wall.

"Will everything be OK?" Eric asked as he looked at his mom with tears in his eyes. "I didn't mean to hurt them. I'm so sorry."

His mother put her arms around him. "Of course, you didn't. It was just a mistake," she comforted. "I think we discovered it in time. Everything will be just fine when you get home from school this afternoon."

When Eric got home from school that day, he raced through the house without noticing the birthday balloons and cake on the dining room table. He ran straight to his room. Throwing his book bag on his bed, he searched the fish tank for signs of his catfish. Nothing. He raced to the kitchen.

"Happy birthday, Eric . . . " his mother started.

"Mom, I can't find Moby," Eric interrupted. "Did he die?"

Eric's mother took her son's hand and led him back to his room.

"See," she pointed. "He's right behind the treasure chest."

Eric stared with relief. Every time the aerator shot out bubbles, the treasure chest opened, revealing the catfish hiding behind it.

Eric gave his mother a hug. "I forgot it was my birthday."

His mother smiled and handed him a large white envelope. They sat together on the couch.

He opened the envelope, pulled out a letter, and read.

Dear Eric:

Welcome to the Whale Adoption Project. On behalf of the humpback whale you have adopted, we thank you. The name of your adopted whale is "Patches": first sighted by the research team in 1980, this famous male has been seen every year since then, except 1991. Spotted in May 1992, he continues to thrill whale watch boats with his breaching and flipper-slapping displays.

Eric looked up at his mother. "Keep looking inside," she said. "There's more."

Eric dug deep inside the envelope. He took out a picture of his humpback whale, a T-shirt, a poster-size whale migration map, and a promise of further updates on his adopted whale.

"This is another animal that is in trouble, Eric," his mother explained, "just like your catfish this morning. People from all over the world are trying to find ways to save this whale and others of its kind."

"Thanks, Mom," Eric said as he hugged her. "I'm going to introduce Patches to Moby." Eric went into his bedroom and replaced the old picture behind his fish tank with the picture of Patches.

Respond to an Environmental Crisis

Purpose: To enable a child to respond to an environmental crisis out of love.

Participants: Lower elementary-age children in small groups or family settings.

Setting: Classroom or home.

Materials: Will vary with the project chosen.

How-To: Knowing a child's particular interest in the natural world—an animal, a bird, or a natural area such as a river or a lake—is the key to this activity.

The first step involves finding a project within the classroom or home that will enable the child to nurture an interest in and love for the natural world. Be aware of ways in which the activity might later be connected to a larger problem (for example, care for an animal may later extend into concern about endangered species; taking care of an aquarium may lead to an awareness of oceanic crises).

Help the child develop responsibility for all aspects of the project, including daily chores. Encourage dialogue about the facts they learn as well as the feelings that are engendered. Expressing feelings is an important link to sustained involvement in this caring project. This part of the activity will take months.

As problems develop (sick animals, diseased or drought-stricken plants), help the child work out solutions to the crisis.

Assist the child in identifying parallel situations in the world at large. In "The Cry of the Sea," the child's aquarium became an avenue that led him to care for whales. His mother took out a membership in the Whale Adoption Project, International Wildlife Coalition, 634 N. Falmouth Highway, P.O. Box 388, Department 93LE, North Falmouth, Massachusetts 02556-0388.

Other Ideas for Responding to an Environmental Crisis

1. Visit a supermarket. Count the many types and brands of bottled waters on the market. Ask the grocer what they sold ten years ago. Ask why? What water quality problems exist in your area that have resulted in the growth of this product? Do local efforts exist to enhance the water quality of your community?

2. Support the survival of the timber wolf and the common loon by writing: The Timber Wolf Alliance and Loon Watch, Sigurd Olson Environmental Institute, Northland College, Ashland, WI 54806.

3. Find out what environmental crises exist in your community by reading the newspaper, listening to radio talk shows, and talking to area politicians and conservation groups. What is currently the most pressing issue? Find out if there is anything you, your family, or your schoolmates can do.

4. If you live in an area with lakes and rivers, go to the bait shops or fishing tackle stores and interview the owner about the status of the fish population and how it has changed or not changed over the years. Encourage the owner to speculate on the reasons for the change. In the Upper Midwest and Northeast areas of the United States and in Canada, acid rain and acid snow may be key factors in declining fish populations.

5. Write a letter to area or national businesses that are responding to environmental crises by altering the way they do business or by changing a product line. Affirm their efforts. Many businesses have ceased using Styrofoam and similar plastic products, found alternatives to testing products with the use of animals, or designed more energy-efficient models.

6. Write the League of Women Voters to obtain a list of the environmental voting records of your senators and representatives. One of the ways to fight environmental degradation is through legislation.

7. Support conservation organizations at local, state, and national levels. Many provide educational resources to encourage a fascination with the earth and outline pathways for its healing.

8. Subscribe to the National Wildlife Federation's magazine for children, *Ranger Rick*. Each issue contains information about various animals in North America as well as a short story depicting responses to environmental crises.

9. Visit a cemetery. Notice stones that were placed over one hundred years ago. Look at the weathering on the stone, the effects of wind, rain, and plant life. Now look for stones placed within the last ten years. What weathering do you see on those stones? Acid rain and snow are produced by coal- and oil-burning power plants, factories, and cars when their emissions mix with clouds. The resulting acid rain and snow damages plants, trees, fish, and water environments. It also eats away stone and metals.

10. If you find an injured creature, a robin or a squirrel, for example, wait for a while to see if its mother or father will attend to it. If no animal or bird appears, care for this wounded creature by calling a veterinarian or a nearby animal or raptor rehabilitation center for advice.

11. Send older children on a propellant hunt. Check kitchen and bathroom cabinets, the garage, and the basement for

aerosol cans. Depletion of the ozone layer has been linked to the use of aerosols. The next part of this task is to go to the supermarket and find alternatives for these products. Make a commitment to care for the earth by changing what you buy.

Did You Know?

Did you know that others beside Eric have responded to environmental crises out of their deep commitment to and love for the earth?

A young boy in France, Jacques Cousteau, learned to love the sea and its fascinating underworld. He spent his childhood on its beaches, then embarked on a lifetime pursuit of ocean depths and the life of the sea.

In his early adulthood, he worked with a Parisian engineer to design an underwater breathing device. Until that time, equipment for underwater exploration had been cumbersome. With the invention of these compressed-air tanks, Cousteau became the world's first scuba diver. In the decade following this invention, Cousteau became convinced that the oceans were rich with natural resources and would provide a wealth of food and energy for humankind. He refurbished a World War II mine sweeper and renamed it "Calypso." Its mission was to study and photograph marine ecosystems.

Cousteau kept both film records and journals about his underwater voyages. He documented his love of the sea by producing films and publishing books about this silent world. In 1966, his work drew national attention with the production of a television series, "The Undersea World of Jacques Cousteau." Audiences were drawn into Cousteau's adventures and discoveries as the world of sharks, whales, coral reefs, underwater frogs, elephant seals, and squids was revealed in the living rooms of people around the world.

When repeating a dive he had made thirty years previously in the Mediterranean Sea, Cousteau made a discovery that would change the direction of his career. While diving in those familiar waters, he and his crew noticed the lack of fish life. Where thirty years earlier they swam among schools of sardines and damselfish, they encountered emptiness. Not a fish swam by them. Local fishermen corroborated their observations. Cousteau's research and programs took on another mission: responding to the crisis in the oceans. He felt that if people could be drawn into the awe and wonder of the natural world, they would also be drawn to protect it. Jacques Cousteau became a champion not only for the underwater world he explored but also for the entire planet. He had discovered that the earth is an interconnected web, intrinsically linked. In *Jacques Cousteau: Champion of the Sea*, he is quoted: "I am reminded that the earth is a living body, an interlocking system of delicately balanced forces, endlessly changing—the sea and the cliff, the tree and the desert."

Mary Hunter Austin, a champion of the desert and its people was born in an Illinois farming community in 1868. Upon her graduation from high school, she traveled to California to homestead. She settled in the Sierra Nevada and fell in love with the desert. She shared that love in two ways: as a writer and an activist. During her lifetime as a novelist, poet, essayist, and playwright, she wrote over thirty-five books and hundreds of shorter works.

Her first book, *The Land of Little Rain*, captures her enchantment with mesquite and mesas: "The secret charm of the desert is the secret of life triumphant." She invited her readers to enter the desert not as a vacation visitor, for its secrets would be withheld. She called them instead to enter the foothills, go beyond the borders and knock at her doorstep. "And there you shall have such news of the land, of its trails and what is astir in them, as one lover of it can give to another."

Austin's depiction of the desert emphasized the harmony between earth and humans. She fought to preserve the balanced way in which native and Hispanic people lived in this land of little rain. The threat of diverting water from the region arose in 1905. Austin fought against this proposal by the Bureau of Reclamation. Twenty years later, she became a delegate to the Seven States Conference, which fought against the diversion of the Colorado River to an expanding Los Angeles. In *The Land of Little Rain,* Austin wrote, "It is difficult to come into intimate relations with appropriated waters; like busy people they have no time to reveal themselves. One needs to have known an irrigating ditch when it was a brook, and to have lived by it, to mark the morning and evening tone of its crooning." Austin's intimacy with the southwest desert, and her love of the land and its people, moved her to respond to environmental crises that would change forever the character of her adopted homeland.

Others on this earth have loved the land upon which they were born and from which they derived a living. Chico Mendes grew up in the Brazilian rain forests of the Amazon. The Amazon rain forest is an intricate web of plant and animal life covering over 2.4 million acres. Scientists have discovered what native people knew for centuries—the incredible diversity of species within this ecosystem: more than 50,000 species of plants, 3,000 kinds of fish, and 230 species of trees which support hundreds of insects. From the time he was nine years old, Mendes's father taught him the delicate balance of living in the Amazon forest as they used its resources, the rubber trees, while sustaining the life of the whole environment. Rubber tappers depend on a healthy forest. They are taught to vary which trees they tap and work different areas of the forest. This ensures the tree's recovery and the continuation of the natives' livelihood.

But others in the forest made their living by destroying it. Logging companies, ranchers, and farmers cut down thousands of acres of forest each year. Expanding populations and rising consumerism led to this destruction. Mendes and other rubber tappers began their fight to save the rain forest with letters to the Brazilian government. They worked with the unions. They began to stage peaceful protests, occasionally forming a human chain around the trees themselves. They formed alliances with people and organizations around the globe, and the destruction of the rain forest became an international issue. Mendes was recognized by the United Nations in 1987 for his efforts to save the rain forest. He was awarded the Better World Society Protection of the Environment Medal. In the course of this struggle, however, Mendes was murdered by the opposition.

Caring for the earth, whether it is the ocean, the desert, or the rain forest, is an act of love, an act of recognition. To live well on the earth in the future, we must care for it today. Cousteau, Austin, and Mendes are three examples of people who cared enough to respond.

Resources

With the Whales by Dr. James Darling. Photography by Flip Nicklin. Minocqua, Wisc.: NorthWord Press, 1990.

Going on A Whale Watch by Bruce McMillan. New York: Scholastic, Inc., 1992.

I Wonder If I'll See A Whale by Frances Ward Wheeler. Illustrations by Ted Lewin. New York: Philomel Books, 1991.

Jacques Cousteau: Champion of the Sea by Catherine Reef. Illustrated by Larry Raymond. Frederick, M.D.: Twenty-First Century Books, 1992.

Chico Mendes: Fight for the Forest by Susan DeStefano. Illustrated by Larry Raymond. Frederick, M.D.: Twenty-First Century Books, 1992.

Helping Our Animal Friends by Judith E. Rinard. Washington, D.C.: National Geographic Society, 1985.

Care of the Wild, Feathered and Furred by Mae Hickman and Maxine Guy. Santa Cruz: Unity Press, 1973.

Save the Earth: An Action Handbook for Kids by Betty Miles. New York: Alfred A. Knopf, 1974 (1991).

EcoNet: The Environmental Computer Network, 18 deBoom Street, San Francisco, CA 94107; 415-442-0220.

Nurture

Remember
to nurture
the earth.

Caring

Sometimes it is easy to care for the earth: filling a birdfeeder on the way to the car or picking up a discarded can while walking along a forest trail.

Sometimes it is not easy. Society often isolates us from the earth. When we are isolated from the earth, it is important to be intentional in showing our care for it.

Follow Tony as he realizes that he can care for the earth even when he is far from the outdoors. Extend your care through careful living. Be a long-distance earth lover.

Far from the Outdoors

"We're going to have to park all the way up in Alaska," Derek called out from the back seat.

"Derek, don't exaggerate," his older brother, Tony, growled from beside him.

"I'm not exaggerating," Derek responded quickly. "Just watch as we go up. The mall is so full today that we'll have to park on the top, and that level is named Alaska. I told you, I'm not exaggerating."

Tony responded with brooding silence.

Their mother broke the silence as she pulled the car into an empty space on the top level of the ramp. "Tony, why don't you just relax and have a good time today. We all know that you would rather be at the cabin this weekend, but this is our only chance to do some back-to-school shopping. There are two more weekends of the summer left. We'll go up north again for both of them."

"I sure would rather be outdoors, Mom," Tony responded as he placed his forehead against the window. "I'm just like Grandpa. I'd rather be on the lake than here in the city. Besides, I don't care if I ever see the Mall of America."

"I appreciate your love of the outdoors, Tony," his mother responded, still smiling. "But I think you should make the best of this trip today." She stood with her other two children outside the car, waiting for Tony. "Besides, Aunt Jenny works here and she's anxious to show us around. We're supposed to meet her at the entrance to Camp Snoopy."

As his younger brother and sister led the way through the hallway from the ramp to the mall, Tony mumbled something about Camp Snoopy being a silly name. He showed absolutely no signs of enjoying himself.

They entered the mall and his mother turned again toward Tony. "Look at the trees, Tony. Feel the moisture in the air. This place is full of nature. It smells like a tropical forest." They were surrounded by large trees. The area was expansive, its roof arching so high that it was hard to tell that they were indoors.

Tony was not impressed. "This place is about as far from the outdoors as a person can get," he stated indignantly. "In fact, it seems to be all about things that are the opposite from the outdoors."

Just as Tony began to elaborate on his last statement, his Aunt Jenny arrived. "What are you all so serious about? Here you stand in the middle of a crowd that's having fun, and you all look like you've received bad news. What's going on?"

Her sister answered first. "The bad news today is that Tony has to be here. He is convinced that he has the undeniable right to spend every summer weekend of the summer up at the cabin. Now he is making sure that his bad news is our bad news."

Jenny looked at Tony and smiled. "I understand, Tony," she said. "I grew up spending my summers at the cabin, and I'd rather be there, too. Your grandfather taught me the joys of life in the north."

Tony was not convinced. "If we all agree that it's so great up there, then why are we all here?" He walked over to a bench and sat down. "Why don't I just wait here while the rest of you go malling?"

The younger kids were drawn by the screams from the roller coaster. "Can we go on some rides?" they asked their mother.

"When our school shopping is done, we'll have some time for that," she replied. "Tony, you need to come, too. We are wasting too much time on your bad mood. Let's go."

Jenny put her arm around Tony's shoulders. "We're connected to the earth right here in this mall. Walk along and see if you can figure out how."

"If it's this so-called tropical forest, I am not impressed," Tony stated flatly.

Jenny remained positive. "The connection to the earth I'm talking about is much more important than just having gardens in the mall, Tony."

Whether it was the mystery of her invitation or a simple acknowledgment of defeat that drew him, Tony joined his family as they headed toward a shopping level.

Derek led the way as they neared North Garden Street, an area designed to create an old-fashioned summer shopping experience. Tony was convinced that his mother made him try on more pants than usual because she was frustrated with him, but he remembered the mystery again as they entered an area called West Market. He was completely stumped. There was no way that he could imagine any important connections between this place and the outdoors that he loved.

"Are you sure you aren't just leading me on, Aunt Jenny?" he said.

"Oh, I'm definitely not leading you on, Tony," she replied, smiling and enjoying the secret.

They were joined by Tony's mother and the two other kids. "Let's go to Camp Snoopy," Beth, the youngest, shouted. "We're all done shopping."

"I'm hungry," Derek said as he looked around for the nearest place to eat.

"Food sounds good to me, too," Jenny added. "Let's find something to eat first, then I'll show you where I work. That will leave the rest of the time for the rides at Camp Snoopy. Besides taking care of our hunger, I think that getting some food might help Tony in solving his mystery."

Jenny led them to a large food court with vendors offering a multitude of international choices. All three kids settled for hamburgers and fries. Tony was hungry enough to forget about solving anything. After the meal, they cleared their tables.

"I'll give you a clue, Tony," his aunt said as they moved toward the trash bins. "You're getting warmer."

"What do you mean?" Tony snapped. "Does it have to do with this recycling? We do this all the time at school. It's no big deal. I don't really see how this has much to do with the outdoors."

As they left the eating area, Jenny led the way. "Follow me and I'll see if I can make some sense out of this for you." Tony dutifully followed his aunt. "We're headed toward the place where I work. I think I can make my point there, but let me begin as we walk."

She paused to let Tony and the other kids catch up. "When Grandpa died a couple of years ago, remember what we all decided to do to help Grandma?"

Tony answered with a question. "Is that when we took over the care of the cabin?"

Jenny stopped to face them. "That's right. When Grandma thought she would have to get rid of the lake property that Grandpa loved so much, we decided that we would take over the care of it. We all do our best to maintain it like they did. It is a way of showing our love for her and honoring the memory of Grandpa."

"We also decided to write letters and call Grandma regularly," Beth added.

"Those are both ways that we show her that we care even when we can't be with her," Jenny responded as they began to walk again. "It's not quite the same, but some of the people who designed this mall love the earth, too. They planned for ways we can show that love even while we are far away from its beautiful places."

As they walked, Jenny pointed to another group of recycling containers. "Recycling is a very important way of showing love for the earth. Over half of the waste in this mall is recycled or reused. Cardboard, glass, paper, aluminum, steel, plastic, and polystyrene are all recycled. Hangers, for example, are reused. All of the tenants are trained about recycling. On the lower level twenty people work full-time in recycling."

"How do you know so much about this stuff, Aunt Jenny?" Derek asked.

As the group approached a store front on the third floor, Jenny answered him. "Because I work right here," she said with pride. "This is the BFI RecycleNow Center."

"What can you sell at a recycle center?" Tony asked.

"We sell very little here," she answered as they sat down on a bench. "This is an education center where mall visitors can learn more about the environment and waste disposal." She patted the bench on which they were sitting. "What do you think they used to make this bench?"

Derek tentatively answered, "It looks a little like gray wood."

Jenny laughed and responded, "It's supposed to look like wood, Derek, but

it's really made out of recycled milk bottles. The carpet is made from recycled soft drink bottles."

Tony was interested. "Is everything in the mall made from stuff that's been recycled?"

"Most of the materials in this center are," she answered. "It is our hope that we can further the cause of using environmentally sound building material through our educational efforts."

"I get your point," Tony said. "Even when we have to be here in the city, we can show our love for the outdoors. The things that we buy and how we throw them away become a kind of letter like those we send Grandma. Right?"

"That's it, Tony," Jenny replied. "Now let's walk through the center, and then we'll head for Camp Snoopy."

Purpose: To establish a recycling program in your home, school, or office.

Participants: Adults and school-age children under their supervision can participate in this activity. If your city or town does not have a curbside recycling program, someone with a driver's license must be involved.

Setting: A basement, back hallway, or storage room.

Care for the Earth

Materials: Sturdy bins to separate glass, paper, aluminum, metal, and plastic trash; twine to bundle paper and cardboard; a can crusher and newspaper stacker are optional.

How-To: Find out what recycling programs exist in your community. More than twenty-six states and many cities and towns have mandated recycling programs. Other communities have centers for voluntary collection.

If your community has a local recycling center, plan a field trip to it. Ask the manager where the recyclables are shipped and what materials are created as a result of their recycling.

Find out which materials can be recycled in your community. Over the past few years, commercial markets have been developed in many communities for the following: newspaper; high grade white paper (typing paper, stationery, computer paper); glass (clear, green, and brown); metal cans (aluminum and bi-metal); unwaxed, corrugated cardboard; motor vehicle batteries; motor oil; plastics (with a recycling number one or two imprinted on the bottom of the container).

In preparing these materials for recycling, paper, cardboard, and newspaper should be bundled or boxed; glass should be separated by color and metal caps and rings removed; metal cans should be separated by type (aluminum and other metal); and plastics should have plastic rings and caps removed. Glass and plastic containers should be rinsed.

Set up your recycling center in a corner of a hallway, storage room, or basement. Place sturdy containers alongside one another to make trash separation handy. After you finish supper dishes or end the day at school or work, assign a member of your family, staff, or class to carry out the recyclables for the day.

As the containers fill, arrange for transportation to a recycling center.

Encourage other friends, family members, schoolmates, or business associates to consider establishing a recycling center.

1. Do a toilet paper turnaround. Colored paper can release toxins. Go to the store and look for white paper. You might consider purchasing recycled toilet paper, facial tissue, and paper toweling.

2. Recycle and reuse shopping bags when going to the supermarket. Brown grocery bags are quite durable and can be reused several times. Another alternative is to purchase sturdy canvas or cloth bags, or make them as a family or school project.

3. Try to purchase items in nonplastic containers. Plastic containers use a nonrenewable resource (petroleum) in their production, and only a few types of plastic currently are recyclable. Be aware of overpackaging on other items. Instead of purchasing individually wrapped items, consider buying in bulk.

4. Buy books and gifts from environmental organizations and agencies or organizations that support indigenous people.

5. Use natural light when possible and low wattage bulbs when bright light is not needed. Replace incandescent lights with

Other Ideas for Caring for the Earth

fluorescent lights. Or contact the local power company to purchase halogen bulbs.

6. Be a smart shopper. Educate yourself with one of the available consumer guides and buy durable products.

7. Recycle clothes when you are finished with them. Pass them along to family and friends. Take them to local thrift shops or secondhand stores. Make worn clothes into cleaning rags, crazy quilts, or blankets for pets.

8. Share newspaper or magazine subscriptions with family and other friends. Encourage the marketing staff of magazines you read to consider using recycled or recyclable paper.

9. Reuse bread bags and other plastic bags that you buy. Wash them in soapy water and hang them on a rack made especially for this purpose. Making and designing the rack could be a good family activity.

10. Talk to those who make purchases for your church, office, school, 4-H club, or scouting organization and encourage them to avoid using Styrofoam containers and products. These products contribute to the depletion of the ozone layer.

11. On your weekly grocery shopping trip, examine what you buy. Before you go to the checkout counter, take note of what containers can be recycled or reused. Contact the city recycling service to determine what products they accept. Find an alternative product for those packages that will end up in the garbage can.

Did you know that you can provide long-term care for the earth by limiting the amount of trash and toxic wastes that you buy and return to the earth.

Products made from toxic substances and those that are over-packaged or that come in throw-away containers are harmful to the earth. Consumers who care for the earth can respond by precycling, making environmentally sound decisions at the store before purchasing products.

Why does an awareness of buying habits and trash generation have an effect on the earth? There are two reasons. One is the problem of space. America's landfills are filling up. It is estimated that by the year 2000, more than half of the landfills will be filled to capacity. The average American produces 3.5 pounds of waste daily. That's up from 2.65 pounds of waste in 1960. The United States generates more waste than any other country in the entire world: 180 million tons of trash annually. Of that, 158 tons are discarded. These resources could be reclaimed and returned to the resource pool.

Therein lies the second reason to become environmentally as-tute consumers. Within ecosystems, resources have cycles in which the raw materials return to the earth and can be reused. Consider the water cycle. Rainfall seeps into groundwater sys-tems. It is picked up by plants which return the water to the atmosphere through transpiration. The water on the earth has been used and reused for 4.5 billion years. Minerals and other elements have similar cycles. But human patterns of resource use have speeded up movement of many materials. Their cycles have become acyclic, resulting in too few nutrients in one place and too many in another. This kind of acyclic process has led to localized air pollution, advanced eutrophication of lake systems, and resource depletion at rates that may not be recoverable. The aim of conservation of natural resources is to make acyclic processes more cyclic.

Currently, only 13 percent of our garbage is recycled. The largest portion of our trash (73 percent) is buried in landfills. Incineration accounts for 14 percent of our garbage disposal and often produces electricity for municipalities. Ocean dumping, which once was popular in many coastal communities, has been banned.

The composition of our solid waste varies from household to household and city to city. On the average, however, 34.2 percent of our garbage is paper products, 20 percent yard waste, 8.5 percent food waste, 7.1 percent glass, 8.4 percent metal, 9.1 percent plastic, and 12.7 percent textiles, rubber, wood, and rubble. These figures do not include wastes from industries, agriculture and animals, abandoned autos, or sewage sludge. If yard and food wastes were composted (a decomposition process that produces a rich soil through the action of bacteria and microorganisms), almost 30 percent of our wastes would be returned to the earth, enriching the soil. If recycling programs were mandated throughout the country, another 25 percent of our waste would be eliminated. Currently, more than half the states, one thousand communities, and six of the largest cities in America have established recycling laws.

Resources

Shopping for a Better World by Alice Tepper Marlin, Jonathan Schorsch, Emily Swaab, and Rosalyn Will. New York: Council on Economic Priorities, 1992.

How To Make the World a Better Place by Jeffrey Hollender. New York: William Morrow and Company, 1990.

50 Simple Things Kids Can Do to Save the Earth by John Javna. New York: Andrews and McMeel, 1990.

Earth Book for Kids by Linda Schwartz. Illustrated by Beverly Armstrong. Santa Barbara, Calif.: The Learning Works, 1990.

Trash Attack by Candace Savage. Illustrated by Steve Beinicke. Buffalo, N.Y.: Firefly Books, 1991.

Green Earth Resource Guide by Cheryl Gorder. Tempe, Ariz.: Blue Bird Publishing, 1991.

Embracing the Earth by D. Mark Harris. Chicago, Ill.: The Noble Press, 1990.

Magazines:

Garbage: A Practical Journal for the Environment. P.O. Box 51647, Boulder, CO 80321-1647.

Greenkeeping: The Environmental Consumer's Guide. Box 28, Annandale-on-Hudson, NY 12504.

Nurture

Remember
to nurture
the earth.

Rest

Sooner or later all living things need rest. It is part of our natural cycle. Children run with seemingly boundless energy and then curl up in their mother's arms for a nap. Caterpillars build a cocoon, a resting place in which they transform into butterflies. The seed for the jack pine rests within the pinecone awaiting its release to become a tree.

As we live in relationship with the earth, sometimes we need to rest in its presence. Take a rest with the earth.

Nothing to Do

"There's nothing to do," nine-year-old Becky sighed. "I'm bored."

It was the twentieth of August. One more week and school would begin, returning Becky to a circle of friends and a busy schedule. Though the summer had been filled with adventures (a rafting trip down the Yellowstone, two weeks at camp, and other shorter trips), the last few days of summer always brought this complaint.

"Why don't you call a friend?" asked her mother, Sarah.

"Megan's out of town," Becky responded flatly.

"How about starting the embroidery project that you got from Grandma for your birthday?" Sarah offered again.

Becky sighed, "I'm not in the mood."

"I know. You can help me pick cucumbers and tomatoes," Sarah teased.

Becky cocked her head and stared at her mother.

"Honey, I've laid out several options for you," Sarah said. "You've got to make up your mind to do something."

"That's right, Mom, I want to do something," Becky replied quickly, "and all I can find is nothing."

Sarah reached out and gave her daughter a hug. "How about taking our bikes out for a ride?"

Becky didn't look thrilled, but she nodded and said, "Maybe I could call Ruth."

Sarah, looking forward to the ride, added, "While you are at it, see if your brother wants to tag along. Maybe you could call some other friends, too."

Less than a half hour later, seven people were cruising along the alleys and back roads of town. Sarah rode behind the neighborhood pack. They toured the local marina and the ironworks and eventually came to the cemetery. This last place, with all of its roads and paths, was a perfect place for races and bike tag. Sarah parked her bike and watched the kids play. She marveled at their energy and endurance.

As the excitement of the game wore off, Sarah challenged the group to a long-distance bike ride out to Houghton Falls. They rode single file along the highway for three miles and then turned onto a gravel road for the last mile. As they parked their bikes, Sarah looked down the pine needle path toward the lake. Red-brown roots clung to the thin soil on top of the sandstone ledge.

However, she was drawn in the other direction, toward a canyon upstream from the falls. The canyon had been carved by the flood waters of the small stream that now trickled along its floor. This spot was little known, even to locals. She had been here with adult friends once. On that visit, Sarah had been impressed with the power of the place—a quiet power that had stilled their voices.

Sarah was hesitant about bringing this not-so-quiet, not-so-adult group into the stillness of this place. Yet she felt compelled to try.

"Hey, Mom," Becky called. "Let's get going."

As they entered the path, Sarah whispered a request for the group to remain quiet as they traveled toward the canyon. She presented it as a challenge. They accepted and walked single file in an uncomfortable silence.

The ground dropped off on the left side of the path, revealing a narrow, deep canyon. On the other side of the canyon, the green of the forest gave way to a brick-colored wall of sandstone. From a depth not yet seen came a hollow trickle announcing life still flowing, still cutting rock. As the group descended along a small ledge, their silence changed, becoming a natural response to the environment. Restful silence was no longer a game. It was, for the moment, their only possible response to the world around them.

They reached the bottom. The air was still, out of reach of the wind that rustled the treetops high above. Sandstone caves with moss carpets opened in front of them and invited entrance to the earth unseen. The world stood still in this ancient place. They were far away from their busy little town. Silently, one by one, they sat . There was nothing more to do. They rested.

Purpose: To rest in the presence of the earth.

Participants: It is preferable to do this activity alone; however, it can be done with families or groups of friends.

Setting: Variable, a quiet place is essential.

Materials: Nothing.

Rest with the Earth

How-To: Allow some time to make the transition between energetic activity and quiet rest. If you are with a group of children, plan a vigorous outdoor activity to expend their energy, a bike ride, a running game, or a hike, for example.

Once you sense the energy of the group subsiding, shift the tone of the outing to one of quiet observation. Challenging older children with a quiet hike, or encouraging younger children to enter the silent world of forest or streamside creatures are both time-tested ways of encouraging a quiet presence.

Walk single file, or sit apart from one another.

Let the spirit of the earth draw you into its presence.

Stay in that place until the uneasiness of the silence fades into a comfortable acceptance.

If it feels right, on the journey home, talk about what each person saw, heard, felt, or thought.

Use the information in the "Did You Know?" section of this chapter to draw connections between your resting with the earth and what happens in the natural world as each living and nonliving thing rests.

Other Ideas for Resting with the Earth

1. Participate in your favorite outdoor activity but change the action of the outing. If you golf, leave out the clubs; if you go fishing, do everything but put a line in the water; if you hunt, leave the gun at home; if you go outside to shoot photographs, leave the camera at home. Go through all the steps

but don't complete the action. Become absorbed in the surroundings rather than the activity.

2. Set aside a time each week to rest with the earth. Be committed about sticking to your schedule. Start out with a half hour then consider increasing the time as you do nothing at all but be present in the natural world.

3. During the winter months, pick a dormant or hibernating animal to adopt as a role model. Learn everything you can about how this particular animal rests during the winter months. Then imagine ways you could mimic this pattern in your life. Try out these ideas.

4. If you're a plant enthusiast, get a Christmas cactus. Watch the plant throughout the year as it goes into its dormant state. During the fall season, water it less often and place it in a cool, dark part of your house (a basement or outside closet). Let the plant rest for a month, or until buds set on the tips of the leaves. When the buds appear, new life is ready to spring forth. Celebrate the gift of rest and the gift of new life as the Christmas season approaches.

5. Sit by a flowing stream where the water tumbles over rapids. Listen to the variety of water sounds. Let the sounds and rhythm of flowing water draw you into a restful state.

6. In summer months, find a soft-bottomed puddle, pond, or stream. First look at it closely, examining any texture or detail on the bottom surface. Pay close attention to the clarity of the water. Then wade in it, barefoot if possible. Having completed your water walk, sit again to watch the settling

process. Watch the clarity return. Watch the particles settle in still water or be carried away in the current of a stream.

7.   On a sunny day, take a nap outside with a preschooler. After lunch, bring a blanket outside and set it down in a shady spot. Be silent. Listen to the sounds of insects, the wind, and the leaves blowing.

8.   Climb a tree. Find a comfortable perch close to the trunk. Sit quietly and observe the world from this perspective.

9.   Take a timed hike with intentional periods of rest and exertion. Begin with a rest period, paying attention to the sounds of the world around you and the sounds of the world within (your breathing and the beating of your heart). After an initial five minute rest stop, walk briskly for fifteen minutes. Rest again for five, repeating the listening exercise. Walk again for fifteen more minutes, listening during this period, too. Complete the hike with a final rest period. Compare the differences between the rest periods and the periods of exertion. Did you hear more of the external world when you were fully rested? Did the nature of the rest periods change as you became tired? Did you hear and see different things while resting and walking? Rest is not always the same. It changes with your needs and your awareness.

Did You Know?

Did you know that the earth rests? As Becky and her friends rested with the earth, they were not alone. Many living things go into a period of dormancy and rest.

Even lakes turn over for a winter's nap. When the air temperature drops, water in ponds and lakes gradually cools. The movement of the water molecules themselves slows down, and the water becomes colder and denser. The molecules pack together more tightly. They become heavier and start sinking to the bottom, flushing the warm water beneath them to the top. The lake has turned over. This new layer cools to thirty-two degrees and freezes in ice crystals. The ice forms a protective cover, a blanket, for the season of rest.

Winter is a time of rest for many plants and animals. Underneath icy ponds, many aquatic animals burrow into muddy bottoms: painted turtles, snapping turtles, and other reptiles; back swimmers, water boatmen, whirligig beetles; and several amphibians. These animals enter a period of their lives when their body processes slow down. They become dormant.

Dormancy begins as plants and animals respond to changes in the length of daylight. This change triggers an instinctual response. As the amount of daylight decreases, animals store food in fatty tissues to function as fat reserves, which will sustain the animal throughout the winter months.

When we think of a long winter's rest, we often think of hibernation. Hibernation is a prolonged period of dormancy. True hibernators have drastic changes in body temperature and in heartbeat and breathing rates. The woodchuck is a true hibernator. Its normal body temperature of 100 degrees Fahrenheit drops to 37 degrees. Its respiration rate slows from 235 breaths per minute to 4 or 6. The woodchuck's heart rate drops from 80 beats per minute to 4 or 5. Other true hibernators include the woodland mouse and some species of bats.

Winter nappers have slight changes in their body processes and remain inactive most of the winter. Occasionally they emerge from dens or nests on warm, sunny winter days. Winter nappers include the bear, raccoon, skunk, and chipmunk.

Insects, too, have dormant periods. They can winter over as adult forms, eggs, or larvae. Some insects hibernate, like the mosquitos which burrow under logs, rubbish, or boards. Mayflies pass the winter in a pupal stage, dragonflies as nymphs. Some insects go into a quiet stage (diapause) that may last all summer and winter. Beetles travel just below frostline to rest; earthworms can burrow as deep as six feet under ground.

Plants also require a period of rest. Herbaceous plants survive by propagating seeds. The seeds themselves rest during the winter, then bring forth new life in the spring. Perennials, like dandelions, die back to the ground, sending nutrients into the root systems. The snow acts like a down coat, wrapping air over the plants and protecting them from the wind.

Winter is a season of rest for the earth, a part of the natural rhythm which sustains life on this planet. In the ancient Middle East, the Canaanites set aside one day each week for rest. Sabbath was a day for quieting the heart. It was a time to limit or abstain from work.

The Hebrew people recognized that creation itself must rest from human activity. They established sabbatical years, when both the community of people and the community of the land and sea gained strength and refreshment through rest. In the fiftieth year, the jubilee year, the land was given a year's rest from agricultural activities and was distributed equitably for the benefit of the whole community. Families were reunited on the land. The land became a source of renewal for the people living in the Middle East, and was given in return a year of rest.

Northern Lullaby by Nancy White Carlstrom. Illustrated by Leo and Diane Dillon. New York: Philomel Books, 1992.

The Goodnight Circle by Carolyn Lesser. Illustrated by Lorinda Byran Cauley. San Diego: Harcourt Brace Jovanovich, 1984.

A Guide to Walking Meditation by Nhat Hanh Thich. Nyack, New York: Fellowship of Reconciliation, 1985.

Resources

Growth

Growth. It's in the plan. Living beings grow throughout their entire lives. This powerful force is at work from conception to death.

Growth occurs naturally, but it does not always occur easily. Sometimes growth is beautiful and easy to accept. Other times it is painful and requires difficult change. Growth never stands still. We grow strong. We grow old. Then finally we grow still. Death is a natural result of growth.

The earth is a living being in a constant state of growth and change. The activities in this section lead you to examine the power of growth. Grow together with the earth.

Karlyn Holman

Growth

Grow
together
with the
earth.

Life

The earth is alive. A force within it continues from minute to minute, year to year, epoch to epoch. This force moves upon and within the earth, causing growth and change. It is the force of life itself.

This powerful life of the earth shakes continents by earthquake and remakes mountains by volcano. This beautiful life grows pine forests and punctuates them with rivers that sing. Life takes on infinite variety and form.

In the following story, an Alaskan tidal pool draws Marla into the many layers of life within it. Join Marla and be aware of this powerful force—life.

The Pool

The rain stopped falling just as Marla parked her car. The sky had been dark with clouds for two weeks. There had only been two days of sunshine in the entire month since she had moved to southeastern Alaska to teach. Still, it was a beautiful place, with mountains, dark green rain forests, and water all around.

Too much water, she thought as she walked toward the beach. *The water of the ocean seems so dark and lifeless. People often talk about loving the smell of the salt sea. I don't think I like it. It smells like dying seaweed. Living on this island makes me feel like I am trapped.* She reached the rocky shoreline and realized that the tide was out. *That explains why the smell is so strong today.*

The water had receded from the shoreline, revealing more rock shelves than she had ever seen. Depressions in the rock had captured salt water, creating a system of tidal pools. Marla put her rain jacket over one of the rocks and sat down to take in the view. *It really is like a postcard,* she thought as she watched a fishing boat making its way toward Ketchikan. The water reminded her of the lakes back home in Minnesota. They weren't as majestic as the sea, but their simple beauty seemed somehow more wholesome to Marla.

The low-tide smell of dead kelp and tidal pools overpowered her. *This place smells like a fish cleaning house.* She stood up to return to her car and drive home on the island's single road. *The smell matches my mood,* she thought as she paused momentarily and looked into the nearest tidal pool. *Salt water. Salt is what makes the Dead Sea dead.*

Suddenly a movement drew her attention. An orange, spiderlike creature darted from one side of the pool to the other. As her eyes followed it, she noticed several dark brown versions of the same creature swimming around the other end of the pool.

How can they live in this little pool? she wondered, forgetting for a moment that this area was covered with ocean twice daily. As she watched the sea spiders, she noticed black, snail-like creatures working their way up the side of the rock. Before she could even wonder what they were, she saw several small, striped worms swimming in the pool. She knelt down to search the pool for more life, forgetting about the smell—and her depression.

A single small fish hovered in the middle of the pool. *He's waiting for the tide to come in again,* she decided. *This little pool is like an ocean aquarium, only it changes its occupants every twelve hours with the tide.* Then she saw a starfish. It lay in shallow water at the other end of the pool. *This is incredible. All of these things alive in this little pool and I have never seen any of them.*

Marla stood up and walked toward her car, pleased with her discoveries. As she drove back toward town, she realized something: those strange new life-forms had produced new life in her.

Purpose: To examine the layers of life on the earth.

Participants: All ages, as individuals or in groups.

Setting: Any area that is resplendent with life—marshes, wetlands, tidal pools, flyways, rain forests.

Materials: Your five senses plus, depending on the area you explore, binoculars, polaroid sunglasses, waders or hiking boots, field guides.

How-To: Stop and observe the area from a distance. Remain quiet for a few minutes and use your senses to isolate signs of life: movements, tracks, sounds.

Proceed slowly and quietly toward the marsh, river, forest, or tidal pool. Continue using your senses. When you are at the edge of the forest or river, maintain a low profile, being careful to avoid throwing shadows over the water or making fast movements. Be still, continuing the search for life signs only with your eyes.

After observing awhile, have one member of your group stand up and wave his or her arms, possibly flushing out fish or other life, while the rest continue to watch.

Discover the Life of of Earth

If you are exploring a river or wetland, step into a shallow area and, remaining low, notice life you hadn't seen before. Examine the shoreline and plants, lift up rocks and see what's beneath them. Notice areas of water flow and eddies.

If you are exploring a forest, approach the area in a similar fashion, being still and observing layers of the forest: the woodland floor, the herbs, the shrubs, and the tree canopy. Turn leaves, rocks, and logs over in search of life. Remember to replace them before you leave.

As you make your observations, be sure to ask questions about anything you don't know or understand. Consult field guides for identification and further understanding of what you are seeing. Attempt to understand any divots, tears, sawdust piles, tracks, or other unusual markings on the ground or trees. These things are often life signs.

Go beyond your observations. Tap into the feelings that are created as you enter more deeply the community you are visiting.

Other Ideas for Discovering the Life of the Earth

1. Use a microscope to examine different samples of water (for example, tap, river, and swamp water) for life-forms.

2. Enter the magic of the spring season by making a calendar that marks the advance of spring in your neighborhood. Spring is a time of rebirth for the earth. Note the birds migrating, the wildflowers advancing, the grass turning green, the temperatures rising, and the rain falling.

3. Watch life grow as you garden. Four to eight weeks ahead of planting time, start seeds indoors as a family project. Set

aside a corner of the garden for each child in your family. Let them design, plant, weed, and harvest it.

4. Follow the fish. Many parts of the country have rivers and wetlands where fish spawn in the spring and fall. Visit them to view the power of this reproductive instinct. Watch trout and salmon jump rapids and waterfalls. To see freshwater species like walleye and bass, visit slow-moving creeks and rivers near a lake that is known to contain these species. Check for spawning fish from dusk to dawn.

5. Sit outside one half hour before dusk and watch the night sky for insects and the bats that feed on them.

6. Create a model of the web of life. Give a ball of string to one member of a small group. Ask the person to start this free-association activity by naming any life-form. He or she then holds on to the end of the string but tosses the ball to another member of the group who must name a life-form that is connected in some way to the first. The second life-form might eat or be eaten by the first, live in it, or in some other way be associated with it. As the names of life-forms are called out, the ball is tossed from speaker to speaker creating a mesh that symbolizes the web of life.

7. Go outside and sit down. Close your eyes and make a list of the life you hear, smell, and touch. Then open your eyes, and continue to list the life that surrounds you.

8. Visit the Platte River in Nebraska to experience the migration of sandhill cranes. Other places to visit wildlife include the Okefenokee Swamp in Florida, the Mississippi flyway, or any wildlife refuge throughout the world.

9. Take a group of preschoolers to a field of wildflowers for an insect hunt. Look for butterflies, spiders, caterpillars, and ladybugs and other beetles.

10. If you live near a trout stream, go there during a mayfly hatch. Evenings in early summer are the best time.

Did You Know?

Did you know that naturalist Rachel Carson thought tidal pools contained the beauty and mystery of the sea in miniature? But the tides do more than create miniature oceans. They bring life to the nation's shorelines. When the twice-daily tides come in, they flood coastal wetlands with fresh supplies of nutrients, making these wetlands the most productive habitats in the world. Estuaries, shallow tidal areas at the mouths of rivers, also are bathed in the rich soils and foodstuffs, but from inland waterways. These wetlands provide feeding ground for migratory birds, wintering grounds for water birds, breeding habitats for fish, crustaceans, crabs, oysters, and waterfowl, as well as nurseries for shrimp and fish. With such abundant resources, coastal wetlands teem with life. When the tide goes out, the shorelines spring to life with crabs and small crustaceans in search of the food left by receding water. Their natural predators, herons, raccoons, muskrats, and people also comb the beaches in search of their next meal.

Where do you find these life-giving places? Coastal wetlands, a mixture of waterways and grasses, are found along the seacoasts, near lagoons, and behind sandbars or barrier islands. The most famous wetland in the United States is the Everglades. Everglades National Park, which is only one fifth of the total wetland area in Florida, includes two thousand square miles of mangrove swamps and saw grass wetlands across the state's southern tip. The largest estuary in the United States is Chesapeake Bay.

Like coastal wetlands, inland marshes and swamps are also filled with life. The slow-moving waters of these wetlands carry nutrients to rushes, sedges, and cattails, and also keep the water aerated for aquatic life. Well-oxygenated waters break down plant materials quickly. This action provides both nutrients for increased plant production and food sources for muskrats, beavers, amphibians, deer, and moose. Because of the abundance of food in a freshwater marsh, these wetlands provide resting, breeding, and wintering grounds for many species, including 2,500 species of mosquitoes. The larval stages of this pesky insect provide food for fish, other insects, and birds who call marshlands their home. A number of fish also spend part of their life cycle in wetlands: bass, walleye, perch, and pickerel.

Few other places offer such an abundance of life as wetlands. When the United States was first settled, there were 215 million acres of wetlands, including millions of acres of marshes, alder thickets, open bogs, and swamp forests in the north woods. While only one half of those wetlands exist today, they still provide the last stronghold of support for 35 percent of threatened or endangered species, including the whooping crane and the American crocodile.

Resources

The Kid's Nature Book: 365 Indoor/Outdoor Activities and Experiences by Susan Milford. Charlotte, Vt.: Williamson Publishing, 1989.

What Happens in the Spring by Kathleen Costello Beer. Washington, D.C.: National Geographic Society, 1977.

Kids Gardening: A Kid's Guide to Messing Around in the Dirt by Kevin Raftery and Kim Gilbert Raftery. Palo Alto, Calif.: Klutz Press, 1989.

The Curious Naturalist edited by Jennifer G. Ackerman. Washington, D.C.: National Geographic Society, 1991.

ABC's of Nature: A Family Answer Book edited by Richard L. Scheffel. Pleasantville, N.Y.: The Reader's Digest Association, 1984.

The Bug Book by Dr. Hugh Danks. Illustrated by Joe Weissmann. New York: Somerville House, 1987.

Growth

Grow
together
with the
earth.

Change

The natural world often appears to be changeless. It is not. The earth
constantly changes and becomes new. Rivers, lakes, mountains, and
glaciers come and go. Grassy meadows become old-growth forests.

Read about Annie in "Red Buffalo" as she witnesses the earth
changing. Welcome each day as an opportunity for change and growth.

Red Buffalo

After spending the entire previous day and most of the night traveling across Minnesota and South Dakota, Carl was finally home. It had been eleven years since he and his daughter, Annie, had visited his family's homestead in western South Dakota. Their last visit had been when Annie was just a baby. Carl had grown up here, along with his parents and grandparents. Sodbusters. Pioneers who had claimed the foot-thick grasslands of the prairie and turned them into a family farm.

Carl watched his daughter run across the farmyard. When Annie reached the edge of the adjoining field, she hunkered down in the waist-high switchgrass that began where the mowing stopped.

"What's the matter, Annie?" her father called out as he walked over to her hiding place.

"I don't know," she answered quietly. "I felt like I needed to hide. It's so wide open out here. Is it always this windy?"

Carl smiled, "The wind is a constant companion out here." Carl drew his hand to his forehead, then smoothed back his long, thinning hair. "Even though I love our home in the north woods of Minnesota, it always feels good to come home to the prairie. Come on and I'll show you around."

Carl put his arm around his daughter and pointed westward. "When my grandparents came to this part of the state, that's all they saw. Miles and miles of grasslands." He walked into the grass and picked a slender stalk.

"What's that?" Annie asked. "It looks like a caterpillar."

"This is bristle grass," her dad answered. "And you're right, the seedhead does look a bit like a caterpillar. It grows in places where people live." They stopped on an overlook. "Look toward the bottom of the valley. Can you see where the brown color turns red? That is foxtail barley. It was named for its red, tail-like head."

"Look, Dad," Annie shouted. "The wind makes the grass move in waves just like water. The foxtails look like a red lake."

Carl led her deeper into the grass. "This is called a mixed grass prairie because so many grasses grow here."

"Does anything besides grass grow here?" Annie asked. "I don't see any birds or animals."

"When I was growing up, I'd listen

to tales of how great herds of buffalo, thousands in number, roamed freely on these prairies. Coyotes, prairie dogs, and other animals called this land their home, too," Carl responded.

"Are they all still here?" Annie asked.

"When the railroads came through and the land was developed for farms, ranches, and towns, many of the buffalo were shot and coyotes were bounty-hunted. They were a nuisance to the farmers' and ranchers' livestock."

They turned to walk downhill and then stopped as they entered an area of shorter grass. Carl looked at the hills with boyish wonder. "Somewhere around here there used to be a prairie dog town. I wonder if they still live here."

As they walked down the hill an area opened to their right, covered with holes and pathways. Carl crouched down. "There it is, Annie," he whispered. "It looks the same as it did years ago."

Carl and Annie sat down about fifteen yards from the nearest burrow. Each burrow was encircled by a raised earthen rim. There were at least two dozen burrows in this prairie moonscape.

"Where are the prairie dogs, Dad?" Annie asked.

Carl squinted into the sun. "Either they have completely abandoned this site or there is a predator near."

"Maybe they are hiding from us," Annie said.

"Usually they don't worry about humans unless they get much closer than we are," Carl responded.

As if on cue, they spotted a coyote. He noticed them immediately and stopped to look at them before he entered the tall grass.

"Is he going to come after us, Dad?" Annie asked.

"No," Carl answered. "He's probably worried about us coming after him. I think that the coyote is just letting us know that he's aware of our presence. Let's walk a while. We'll stop on our way back to see if the prairie dogs have come out again."

"What's that bird?" Annie asked as she pointed skyward and followed the flight of a golden-colored bird. It dove, then circled slowly about six feet above the ground.

"That's a kestrel," he answered. "We've got those back home in Minnesota. He's hunting for lunch, looking for either field mice or grasshoppers. By the sound of things around here, I'd guess he is feeding on grasshoppers." Carl stood still for a minute. "Listen to that whistling sound. It's been in the background the whole time that we have been out here. That is the sound of thousands of grasshoppers."

Annie looked mildly surprised. "I

hadn't noticed that sound. I guess I heard it, but I wasn't paying attention to it. Now it's so obvious."

They continued walking down the hill toward the bottom of the valley. "Are there any other animals around here, Dad?" Annie asked.

"This hillside used to be covered with jackrabbits," he responded. "They have always been my favorites. We'll kick one up sooner or later. Do you know why jackrabbits have such big ears, Annie?"

"Because they're rabbits," Annie replied with a tolerant smile.

"Very funny," Carl said with his own smile. "Keep guessing."

"It's obvious, Dad." Annie feigned frustration. "Rabbits have large ears for hearing. That way no other animals can sneak up on them."

"That's a part of it, Annie," Carl said. "But there is more." He reached down and picked a single stalk of timothy, placing it between his teeth. "Jackrabbits have exceptionally long ears because they live in prairie and desert regions. They spend long months in hot weather with no place of real shelter. Their ears act like the radiator on our car. They help to release body heat and to keep the rabbits cool."

They turned and started back toward the house. "Are there any wildflowers here?" Annie asked.

"Early in the season there are some, but not many," Carl answered. "The grasses have such strong and intensive root systems that it is hard for seeds to get started. The most common flower is purple prairie clover. It sends its roots deeper than the grass roots, so it doesn't have such strong competition."

Annie ran ahead, shouting a challenge. "I'll race you to the prairie dog town."

"I'll catch up with you there, Annie," Carl shouted after her. "Then we'll head back to the house."

After lunch with Carl's brother, Ted, who lived on the farm, Annie stood up from the table. "I'm going to watch the prairie dogs again. Maybe I'll see a jackrabbit this time."

Carl leaned toward the window, pulled the curtain back, and looked to the west. "Keep an eye on the weather. It looks like there might be a storm moving in."

Annie heard the screen door slam behind her as she ran toward the hills. The strength of the sun reminded her of warm days at home on the lake. *I'm glad the wind is blowing so hard,* she thought, *or else it would be unbearably hot today.*

By the time she reached the prairie dog town, the wind had cooled. *Dad was right,* she admitted to herself. *It really looks like a storm.* She stood to watch the tall purple-black thunderheads swell in waves across the entire western horizon. As she turned to head home, she was surprised to see her father nearby. "Annie, this is looking pretty rough. You'd better come back with me."

As they both looked to the west, light severed the sky. Two sharp lines of green-white lightning left separate places on the same cloud and joined to strike the ground on the other side of the valley. Thunder crashed at the same instant, indicating that the lightning strike was close.

"We'd better run," Annie said as she took the first steps.

When they reached the house, they saw Carl's brother, Ted, plowing between them and the house. When Carl saw the plow, he turned around. "Look, Annie," he said excitedly, pointing toward the horizon. "The lightning we saw started a prairie fire. With this strong wind, it will travel fast."

Annie was interested in Ted. "Why is he plowing when this storm is coming?" she asked. "That doesn't make any sense."

"He's making a firebreak," Carl explained. "If this fire comes our way, it could burn down the whole farm. Ted will plow an area around the farm wide enough to prevent the fire from jumping. That way it will go around us."

Annie pointed down the valley.

"Look, Dad, there are flames. It looks like a moving wall. A red wall."

"The Lakota thought so, too," he replied. "They often saw huge herds of buffalo moving across these hills. These walls of fire reminded them of a buffalo herd, so that's what they called a prairie fire: Red Buffalo. When we saw the lightning strike, we saw the birth of a red buffalo. Now let's move in behind Ted's firebreak and watch the red buffalo travel."

Annie stood between her father and her uncle as they watched the fire. Carried on the wind, the smoke reached them first. The smoke left a sharp bitterness in her nose. It smelled very different to her from the oak, pine, and birch that they burned at home. Then it hit her. "What about the animals?" she screamed. "Will this fire kill all of the animals?"

"It won't hurt most of them," her dad comforted, "but it will be a disaster for the grasshoppers and the mice. The grasshoppers will have little left to eat and the mice will have nothing in which to hide for a time. The prairie dogs go underground. The jackrabbits and coyotes run ahead until the fire wall thins and then jump back."

The fire traveled quickly and was far past them within half an hour. "This is awful," Annie said as they walked over the black soot that covered the ground. "This doesn't even seem like a prairie any-more," she lamented. "There is no grass and I can't see any animals. It's like the prairie died today."

Carl smiled gently. "It looks like the prairie died today, Annie, but in fact this is what allows the prairie to continue. Without fires or droughts the prairies and grasslands would become forests."

Annie searched the blackened ground, trying to figure out what her father was saying.

"All the underground roots will send up fresh grass," Carl continued. "But the trees and nonprairie plants that had begun to grow have been destroyed by the fire. Today, the birthing of the red buffalo brought a change; new life has come again to the prairie."

Explore Change

Purpose: To explore a place of change or transition in the natural world.

Participants: This activity works best with upper-elementary age children who have the ability to notice subtle differences or changes in the plant world. It works best one-on-one, but can be done as a guided naturalist hike with school children.

Setting: Fields, forests, bogs, vacant lots, shorelines, and transition zones between roads and forests or fields. Environmental learning centers often have three or four habitats to explore on their property.

Materials: Camera, field lens, sketch pad, pencil, field guide.

How-To: Read the story "Red Buffalo." Pick out details that describe the natural area Annie was discovering and talk about how the fire changed that environment.

Think about other events that cause the land to change: volcanic eruptions, floods, logging, expansion of city limits, farming.

Discuss what the ecosystems were like before the changes. Describe what they are like now.

Agree upon one natural area you would like to explore for change. This will be a field investigation, using cameras or sketch pads to record overall landscape design and field lenses and guides to help individuals identify members of the plant community.

Begin the investigation by looking at the overall landscape, attempting to identify transition zones. If you are at a lakeshore, you might note where beach grasses appear in the sand and where the grasses are replaced by shrubs and trees. If you are studying the edge of a road, walk from the blacktop toward the forest or field, noting changes in plant life, from grasses and wildflowers to shrubs and trees.

Use a field guide to identify plants you find in each area.

When you return home or go back to the classroom, continue your investigation. The Sierra Club has a series of naturalist's field guides that describe various plant communities and the animal populations within those communities. Compare the descriptions in these guides to your field investigation. Find out what stage comes before and after the plant community you investigated. If possible, discover what existed in that place fifty and one hundred years ago. Contact the county extension agent to view plat books from those times.

1. Go to a nursing home to interview elderly residents of your community, or talk to your grandparents, about how the land has changed over the years. How has their relationship with the outdoors changed?

Others Ideas for Exploring Change

2.   Research the changes that have occurred on the land where you live, from its emergence from primordial seas to the present time. Reading the first chapter in a James Michener novel may help you with this activity. Draw a time line with pictures, noting the major changes.

3.   Experience the changes of the fall season with a child. Go on a leaf-collecting tour in a park or in your backyard. Pick up green, yellow, red, and orange leaves. Bring them home and press them between waxed papers.

4.   Examine how human use of the land in your neighborhood has altered a plant community. Read the accompanying "Did You Know?" in this chapter for more information.

5.   Stand at the edge of a forest and note the plants and trees around you. Walk five feet into the woods, then stop and look for differences. Repeat this activity four times. Does the forest change as you travel deeper into the woods?

6.   Visit a prairie restoration area. Find out how the land managers are maintaining the area.

7.   Research the history of your community. Why was it founded? What was its economic base? How has that economic base changed? In what ways have people had to change in order to live there?

8.   On your child's birthday, plant a tree in your backyard. Each year visit the tree as part of the child's birthday celebration, noting changes in height, girth, and development. Take a picture each year and place it in your child's album.

9.   Find examples of four stages of plant succession: an open field with flowers and grasses, an old field with shrubs and young trees, a young forest, and a mature forest. Note differences in light, soil temperature, moisture, and the layer of humus.

10. Remember a natural area that was a favorite when you were growing up, one that you enjoyed when you were a teenager and young adult, one that you shared with family and friends. Have these places changed since you last spent time there?

Did you know that fire changes the earth but does not destroy it? Annie's father helped her understand that change was necessary to preserve the prairie.

Since land began to emerge from the primordial waters billions of years ago, the natural world has been in a constant state of change. The evolution of plant and animal kingdoms is a testament to the adaptability of living creatures.

Some changes take place over eons, others are much more rapid. Walk into a forest and look for an old stump. Get down on your hands and knees to examine the new life forms: lichens, mushrooms, ferns, and tree seedlings that are springing up from the remains of the tree. Grasslands become forests. Open lakes become meadows. Pine forests reach maturity, then give way to yellow birch and hemlock forests. Nature changes continually.

Perhaps the most dramatic evidence of nature's power to change and adapt was documented in Indonesia, where a volcano on the island of Krakatoa erupted in 1883. Within the first year after

Did You Know?

the cataclysm, grasses and other pioneer plants were struggling to break through the lava. Fifty years later, scientists found the island completely vegetated with species very similar to those on surrounding islands.

Succession is a less dramatic process of natural change. As plants grow they change the habitat by creating more shade and by contributing nutrients to the soil. The acid soils of a pine forest give way to the more alkaline soils of a broad-leaved forest as plants, shrubs, and trees die and decompose. The diminished sunlight in the forest allows shade-tolerant plant species to invade territory previously occupied by light-seeking species. Raspberry, blueberry, and blackberry plants require sunlight to produce their fruits in the summer months, so very few of these shrubs can be found in dark, moist, mature forests.

As competition for sunlight, water, and nutrients builds, new groups of plants dominate. As vegetation changes, animal populations also change because different types of food and shelter are available. Savannah sparrows and goldfinches are found in fields. As shrubs begin to invade these meadows, field sparrows and yellowthroats begin to dominate. In a forested area, thrushes and blue jays are common.

Most changes in nature take time. Scientists who study volcanoes must wait years to see the succession of vegetation that follows an eruption. It is possible, however, to observe successional changes over space rather than time. From the shore of a lake, the succession of beach grasses, pea plants, shrubs, and pine trees can be seen in clear zones from the water's edge inland. Bogs are another plant community where transitional zones are apparent. The center of the bog may be open water encircled by sphagnum mat, larches, and spruce trees. Old homesteads, vacant lots, and old roadbeds are other places to explore changes in plant and animal communities.

The kind of community that develops depends on a number of factors: climate, soil type, elevation, slope, and past land-use activities. Humans have played a significant role in the changes sustained in natural communities. The original mature forests of the North American continent fell to saw and ax as land was cleared for farms and cities. Populations of both plants and animals have fluctuated, depending on our use of them. The destruction of rain forests is another example of how human actions significantly impact natural ecosystems. Fortunately, forestry practices are changing as biodiversity becomes a land management ethic.

Resources

The Curious Naturalist edited by Jennifer G. Ackerman. Washington, D.C.: National Geographic Society, 1991.

ABC's of Nature: A Family Answer Book edited by Richard L. Scheffel. New York: The Reader's Digest Association, 1984.

Man's Mark on the Land: The Changing Environment from the Stone Age to the Age of Smog, Sewage, and Tar on your Feet by Arthur S. Gregor. New York: Scribner, 1974.

Let's Discover the Floor of the Forest by Ada and Frank Graham, Jr. New York: Golden Press, 1974.

Animals in Cities and Parks edited by Dr. Charles P. Milne, Jr. Milwaukee, Wisc.: Raintree Publishers, Inc., 1988.

Urban Roots: Where Birds Nest in the City by Barbara Bash. San Francisco, Calif.: Sierra Club Books, 1990.

Changes in the Land: Indians, Colonists, and the Ecology of New England by William Cronon. New York: Hill and Wang, 1983.

American Prairies by William K. Smithey. New York: Gallery Books, 1990.

Growth

Grow
together
with the
earth.

Death

Life and death are entwined. Each living being must die, but the force of life continues. Life flows from creature to creature, from creature to earth, from earth to creature.

In "A Shooting Star," Adam and Annie are confronted with death. Read how their mother leads them from fear to understanding. Then seek to accept death as a transfer of life.

A Shooting Star

"Mom, look what we found," six-year-old Adam called out as he and his twin sister, Annie, ran toward their mother, Jean. Annie cradled a bright blue bird's egg in her hands.

"Is it a bluebird egg?" Annie puffed, winded from the run.

"No, Annie," Jean replied. "That's a robin's egg. Where did you find it?"

"It was lying right in the path," Adam answered. "There were a bunch of branches with it."

"It must have blown down in last night's storm," Jean concluded. "Was the nest on the ground?"

The kids answered together, "No, we could see it in a tree."

"It was too high to reach," Adam finished for them.

"Can we keep it in our tent and hatch it, Mom?" Annie asked.

"Don't be silly," Adam answered. "We have to figure out how to put it back in its nest."

Jean took the egg and held it to her cheek. Then she knelt down and met the children's eyes. "It's too late for this egg, kids. It's cold. It must have been on the ground all night. Let's just set it back in the woods. A raccoon or another animal might eat it."

"But what if we warm it up again?" Annie pleaded. "Maybe the baby bird inside isn't dead."

"Annie, sometimes it's just too late to do anything." Jean put an arm around each child's shoulders and led them toward the woods.

After lunch they set out on a hike. This was the third time that the threesome had camped in this northern Wisconsin park, and Annie and Adam chose their favorite part of the park to visit: the falls. They led the way, managing to stay just one bend in the path ahead of Jean, but as Jean stepped into a shady glen, she saw them both standing and waiting for her.

"Can we eat these berries, Mom?" Adam asked, his hand full of red berries.

"Where did you get them?" Jean questioned.

"Right over here, Mom." Adam led her to a dark green vine with heart-shaped leaves.

"Those berries will make you sick," Jean replied. "They're called deadly nightshade. But we might be able to find some wild raspberries."

"What good are these red ones if we can't eat them?" Adam asked.

"You can't eat them, Adam, but the birds can. That's one of the wonderful things about the forest. It holds different foods for different creatures," Jean continued. "Every creature has its own diet. If they all ate the same things, the weaker ones would starve."

The berries went flying and so did the kids. They were off to the falls. Jean called after them, "Don't go near the falls until I get there." She walked quickly, but the kids were soon out of sight. She could hear the falls in the distance.

As Jean rounded the last corner leading down to the falls, Annie ran toward her crying, "Mom, hurry. There's an animal lying on the path. It's all bloody."

Adam followed close behind. "I think it's a deer. Come and see."

Adam and Annie led Jean down the path. She stopped after twenty yards. "It *is* a small deer, Adam," she said softly. "It must have been about one year old." Bits of the deer's hair were scattered around the carcass. The steep walls of the sandstone canyon had provided no escape for the cornered animal. Jean turned toward her children. "It must have been caught by coyotes last night. The deer had no place to run away back here."

"Why were the coyotes so mean, Mom?" Annie asked. "He was just a baby."

"They weren't mean, Annie," Jean replied. "They were just eating. Remember the red berries? They are food for birds. The deer are food for coyotes. For one creature to live, another must die."

"I don't like it," Annie said. "Look at how awful it looks."

Adam walked down the trail toward the deer.

"Don't go any closer," Jean called out. "If the coyotes smell humans around this kill, they might stay away, and the food will go to waste. Let's head back toward the campsite and find something else to explore."

The rest of the day passed quickly with a long visit to the lakeshore. In the evening Jean cooked macaroni and cheese as the twins tended the fire, poking sticks into the low flames. The threesome sat silently, listening to the crackle of the fire as biscuits turned golden brown in the reflector oven. The day drew to a close as they ate.

"You two should crawl in the tent now," Jean said. "It's getting late and we've got two more days here."

"Look," Adam shouted, pointing toward the sky.

"I saw it, too," his mother said. "A shooting star. Did you see it, Annie?"

Annie nodded. "Is that a star that just died, Mom? One of my friends said that a shooting star was somebody's sun that fell out of the sky."

Jean smiled. "No, Annie. Most of the shooting stars that we see are meteors. They're left over from the creation of our sun and its planets. They float in space and then burn up when they come near the earth. They're a sign of the beginning of life, not the end."

"You mean that it's not something else that's dead?" Annie said. "I'm glad. I'm tired of dead things."

Jean smiled and held Annie close to her side. "Yes, we've seen plenty of death today. But we've seen life, too: the life of the woods, and the lakeshore, and signs of animal life. Where there is life, there must be death. They exist together."

Examine Death as a Part of Life

Purpose: To examine death in the natural world.

Participants: Any age may participate. The activity leader will need to decide how much of the activity to use, based on the ages and sensitivities of the individuals.

Setting: Any place where death can be encountered, for example, a forest, a city park, a highway, a lake, an ocean.

Materials: None.

How-To: Be prepared to lead this activity when the opportunity arises, taking note of a dying part of the natural world, examining it, and then making connections to broader ecological concepts.

Death can be encountered at any time in the natural world. While driving on a highway, draw attention to a road kill—a bird, a raccoon, a deer, a porcupine, or a squirrel. In the forest, a rotting log can provide the springboard for observation and discussion.

Disturbed nests, bones, or animal skeletons are other signs of death. Death is also often encountered along windward shorelines, where dead fish, birds, insects, and empty shells collect. Hunting and fishing provide other opportunities for examining the place of death in the web of life.

With toddlers, observation is all that is necessary. Don't dwell on death, just observe it, then talk about examples of life. With lower-elementary-age children, move beyond observation and draw out their feelings. Again, make this a quick interaction and move on to other aspects of life. With upper-elementary-age children, teenagers, and adults, the following extension can be added.

Encourage participants to sit in a small group and share stories of death that touched their lives. This may be the death of a human, a wild animal, or a pet. Give ample time for the stories to come out. When the stories have been told, review them by discussing the emotions people had. Did they feel sadness? Pain? Sorrow? Was fear a part of the experience? Were emotions such as joy, love, and respect expressed in their stories? Use this time to discuss death as the following: an enemy, something to fear, a result of growth, a transfer of life.

Other Ideas for Examining Death as a Part of Life

1. Visit a grocery store and talk about the food chain. What plant or animal died to provide some of your favorite foods? What died to provide food for your food?

2. Create a compost pile of kitchen and yard wastes to add to the garden soil. Grass clippings, kitchen wastes (except meat scraps), and manure will decompose as they interact with water, air, and time. These waste products will help plants grow better. You will be participating in the transfer of life.

If you have a vegetable or flower garden, add your compost to it. If not, give the compost to a neighbor or public park site manager.

3. Find a road kill near your home. Watch animals and birds feed off the carcass. Even the bald eagle is a scavenger who gains food and sustenance from dead matter.

4. Write to the Office of Endangered Species, Fish and Wildlife Service, U.S. Department of the Interior, Washington, D.C. 20240 for a list of endangered and threatened species. Learn about an endangered or threatened species that lives near you. What kind of habitat does it need to survive? Why is it endangered? What is being done to assist its recovery? What can you do to help?

5. Hike into a pine plantation or another area where a single plant species predominates. Note which animals, birds, and plants live there. Take another hike to a mixed forest or grassland, again noting the animals, birds, and plants. Compare the number and diversity of species in each area. Which species found in a diverse environment are missing from land managed for one species?

6. Find a dead log in a shaded part of the forest. Look closely and count the number of life forms on it. Are there green plants? Are there other types of growths on it? Look under it. Is anything growing or living underneath?

7. Choose a favorite animal. Find out where it fits in the food chain. What does it eat to survive? What animals depend on it for food?

8.   Be intentional about honoring the lives that are lost in order to provide your food. Some people mention these creatures in a table grace, others are quietly thankful and respectful.

9.   Spend a clear evening counting falling stars.

10. If you fish, consider a catch-and-release method of fishing. Artificial baits are best for this because the fish are usually just hooked in the mouth. Be sure to handle the fish with wet hands and stabilize them in the water until they can swim away. It is all right to keep some fish for a meal or two, but catch-and-release methods protect the fishery for the future.

11. Read about Lake Erie. This lake was dying from advanced eutrophication and pollution, and is currently recovering. Try to find a local example of a waterway that is dying from pollution (human wastes, acid rain, agricultural runoff).

12. Talk with farmers about the life and death cycle as it is seen on their farms.

Did you know that death isn't always bad? When Adam and Annie came upon the dead deer, they began a lesson about life and death.

Life and death are closely entwined. A dead and decaying log teems with life. Biologists estimate that the average decaying log houses twenty thousand creatures. One-third of all forest species live in fallen trees, including chipmunks, salamanders, and carpenter ants.

Did You Know?

As moisture begins to rot a fallen tree, plant pioneers move in to claim its nutrient-rich fibers. Microscopic rootlets of fungi weave a web underneath the bark, eventually sprouting a variety of mushrooms and other fruiting bodies. Mosses cover the log with a lush carpet. Lichens, which are really two plants, an algae and a fungus supporting one another in a symbiotic relationship, also contribute to this vital plant community. As the log decays, the resulting soil provides a rich environment for tiny seedlings of nearby trees to take root alongside the woodland flowers given light by the opening in the forest canopy.

In the Pacific Northwest, rotting logs and old growth forests of Douglas fir and Sitka spruce provide habitat for another species: the northern spotted owl. Over the past decade, this threatened bird has symbolized the fight to preserve both individual species and their habitats. The question raised is how can humans continue to live on the earth alongside other species who are dependent on the same resources, in this case, timber? Loss of habitat to agricultural development, logging, cattle grazing, pollution of air and water resources, and settlement is the most common threat to a species' survival.

Since 1600, more than two hundred species of mammals and birds have become extinct. Extinction means that an entire species no longer exists. While extinction is a natural part of the life cycle of this planet, the rate of extinction concerns scientists. Biologists estimate that 90 percent of all species that ever lived are now extinct. They currently estimate that one of the world's five to ten million species becomes extinct every day, and they are concerned that the rate may be increasing to one every hour.

The great auk, the Atlantic gray whale, the passenger pigeon, Steller's sea cow, and the giant sea mink are extinct. The grizzly bear, the timber wolf, and the bald eagle are threatened with extinction or endangered. Some species, such as the California condor, no longer exist in the wild but are preserved only in refuges or zoos. As of 1992, 1140 species were on the worldwide endangered list. Of the 618 listed in the United States, 38 percent were declining and 2 percent were probably extinct. In Canada, 44 species of animals were designated as threatened or endangered.

In 1973, the United States passed the Endangered Species Act. The act set up a system for identification of endangered species and development of specific recovery plans. An additional purpose of this act was "to provide a means whereby the ecosystems upon which endangered and threatened species depend may be conserved." While the act provides some protection for both plant and animal species, close to four thousand plants and animals are waiting to be listed and there are no current preservation plans for them.

In all of these cases, the maintenance of plant and animal diversity on this planet is at stake. Species do not exist in isolation from one another. Survival of one species is dependent on survival of a variety of other plants and animals. Everything is interconnected. Biodiversity is one measure of the ability of an ecosystem to survive change. The future of the earth rests in that ability.

Death of an individual plant or animal is a natural part of growth. Premature death of a species or habitat is not. With the destruction of the world's most diverse ecosystems, rain forests, perhaps 25 percent of the earth's biota are at serious risk of extinction within twenty to thirty years. The preservation of diverse habitats has become a top priority for the United Nations Environmental Programme. Let it also be yours.

Resources

The Kids' Environment Book: What's Awry and Why by Anne Pedersen. Sante Fe: John Muir Publications, 1991.

The Dying Sea by Michael Bright. New York: Gloucester Press, 1988.

And Then There Was One: The Mysteries of Extinction by Margery Facklum. San Francisco: Sierra Club Books, 1990.

Our Endangered Planet: Rivers and Lakes by Mary Hoff and Mary M. Radgen. Minneapolis, Minn.: Lerner Publications Company, 1991.

Nature's Clean-Up Crew: The Burying Beetles by Lorus J. Milne and Margery Milne. New York: Dodd, Mead and Company, 1982.

Saving Our Animal Friends by Susan McGrath. Washington, D.C.: National Geographic Society, 1986.

Reconciliation

Where there are two living things, there will be difference. Where there is difference, there will be occasional conflict. Where there is conflict, there will be brokenness.

Brokenness can mark the end of a relationship or it can mark the beginning of something new. Reconciliation and renewal are both results of brokenness repaired.

Many human beings do not live in total harmony with the earth. We often have projects and purposes that conflict with the well-being of the earth and break our relationship with it.

In this section the stories and activities are designed to assist you in recognizing broken relationships with the earth and to move you toward attitudes and actions of reconciliation.

Reconciliation

Become
an
earth
healer.

Brokenness

A scar tells a story of pain or injury. Many of us have scars that remind us of childhood bike tumbles.

The earth also has scars. Some of these scars are so commonplace that we don't even notice them.

Read of Karen and her family as they discover a scar on their land. Then seek to recognize the scars that you and your family leave on the earth. Recognition is the first step towards reconciliation.

A Scar

Karen woke up. The house was dark. She turned on the light by her bed. Three A.M. She looked across the hall toward the bedrooms of her two children. The house seemed cold. She threw on her bathrobe and pulled wool slipper socks over her feet. *I'd better check the fire downstairs.*

Before going downstairs to check the wood furnace, she walked across the hall to pull the comforters over her children. The wind howled outside. She could hear it now. A pine branch brushed against her son's window.

Once downstairs, she opened the firebox and stirred the coals. The radiant heat felt good. She tossed in a few more logs from the woodpile, then opened the damper wider. *Something must be happening outside,* she thought.

When she went upstairs, she gazed out her window. Then she saw it. Snow. Not just the flurries that the weatherman predicted. The trees sagged as snow piled on top of each branch. Karen turned off the light to try to get a few hours' sleep before a day she would surely have to spend indoors with two snowbound schoolchildren.

"Mom," nine-year-old David hollered from his bedroom. "Look what happened last night." He ran to his mother's room, and they both gazed out the window. The car was buried in at least a foot and a half of snow. The driveway had disappeared altogether.

David raced to his sister's room. "Becky, wake up," he screamed. "We finally got our wish." Becky rubbed her eyes as David pulled her to the window. "Let's get our snowsuits on and go outside."

Karen smiled. "That's right, honey, there'll be no school bus coming down our driveway today. We're snowed in."

"Hurray," David shouted and danced up and down.

Karen's children had waited all winter for a blizzard. Blizzards meant an extra play day in the middle of the week. The radio announced the elementary school closing as Karen set hot cocoa and oatmeal in front of her children. "It's official," she said.

Ten minutes later, David and Becky were out the front door, climbing three-foot high snowdrifts to the shed to get out their sleds. Their earth-bermed home provided a ready-made sliding hill on the north side of the house. Karen watched from the front door. Their joy was contagious. She set the breakfast dishes aside, dressed for the outdoors, and joined her children sailing down the slopes. After a few trips down the hill, a slippery trough was carved into the snow. *Snow otters,* Karen thought.

"Hey, Mom, look at me," David called. "The great David Carrington will now do his amazing diving feat." He stood up in the sled, held the rope taut and rode the waves of snow down to the bottom, where he flipped into the snow bank. Each descent produced another huge divot in the snow as he laughed through snow-covered eyes.

"I'm going to walk up the road," Karen said to her kids. "See you in a bit." Karen started up the driveway, but she turned back to the house after a few laborious steps. The overnight blizzard had dumped two feet of snow. *Time for snowshoes,* she concluded. Instead of walking back to the shed for snowshoes, however, she sat in the snow, leaned back, and made a snow angel. She laughed. *I haven't done this since I was a little girl.*

Karen gazed up into the trees. The wind had died and the trees swayed only slightly, keeping the mounds of snow high in the branches. She felt a special kinship with the pines. They were what had attracted her to buying this land. She gazed back at the house. Every night before she went to bed, she looked out at the twin pine trees standing near her bedroom window. She watched the golden needles drop in the spring and fall, watched the snow pile up in the winter, and watched the chickadees and blue jays sit in its branches to wait their turn at the bird feeder.

The roar of a nearby engine startled her. *That must be the snowplow.* She glanced up the driveway. "Kids, come quickly. The snowplow's here." Flashing orange lights reflected off the snow banks. A moving mountain of snow broke in front of the road grader.

David and Becky dropped their sleds and ran to her side. This was another favorite part of a snow day. They all walked back to the front porch to watch the magic of a road appearing where none could be seen a few minutes earlier. Three-foot drifts were pushed aside and became ten-foot mounds of snow as the plow cleared the driveway. The kids jumped up and down with delight, cheering for the snowplow. One final swipe and the snowplow turned to leave, clearing the other half of the driveway.

Karen walked up the road, gliding on the now glassy surface. The snowplow had pushed most of the snow away from the side of the car, but it had been a tight squeeze between the car and the pine trees. Karen walked over and began to shovel the snow around the tires. After fifteen minutes of hard work, she turned and leaned against the car to catch her breath. The last wisps of a blizzard wind swirled snow around the pine tree.

The beauty of that moment was broken as Karen stared at the base of the tree. She dropped her shovel and ran over to the tree. The snowplow blade had carved a deep gash into it. She took off her glove and reached out to place her hand over the wound. Sap was running, she felt the stickiness on her hand. She could smell the fresh pine scent, and yet she thought of blood.

Just then the kids came to her side. "What's the matter, Mom?" David said. "You look upset."

"The tree is bleeding," she answered him. "It was cut as the plow cleared around the car."

Becky reached out to touch the tree, too. "Is it going to die?" she asked her mother.

Karen stepped away from the tree and answered her. "No, I think it will survive. The sap that's running now is a natural bandage for the tree's wound. It will carry a scar, though."

"Why do you feel so bad about it, Mom?" David asked. "You didn't do it."

Karen paused thoughtfully, then replied, "It was done for us. It was done so that we can live here. Even though we didn't drive the plow, it's our scar, too."

David looked at her with frustration. "We couldn't keep it from happening, Mom. It was just one of those things."

"We couldn't help it, David," Karen replied, "but we need to notice it. As we live with the earth, we will hurt it, even if we try not to."

David replied, still frustrated, "What are we supposed to do then, feel bad all the time?"

"No," Karen answered. "We need to recognize the broken part of our relationship with the earth and then learn to be healers."

Recognize Brokenness

Purpose: To recognize the scars that we leave on the earth through our individual and corporate activities.

Participants: Families, a group of five or six friends, or a small class (ages ten and up).

Setting: Neighborhood or town.

Materials: A means of transportation (car, bikes, feet).

How-To: Make a game of identifying earth scars in your immediate surroundings. Tour your neighborhood or town while looking for signs of scars or the objects and activities that create them. Many things we routinely see are actually earth scars: a broken branch, a tree stump, tire ruts, spilled gasoline or oil, untended landfills, and erosion.

Look in alleys and around industrial buildings, schools, and stores. Continue your search and then consider the scar-making potential of the area.

Build a story as to how the scars got there, who made them, and what the area looked like before the scar was made.

1.   Tour your home and look for environmental impacts that reach beyond the walls of the house. Many things that we routinely do within our home have an impact that reaches a long distance. Flick a light switch and talk about the impact of that action. Where is the energy made? In what form is it made? How long will it be until the impact of making that energy disappears?

2.   Look in the refrigerator and cupboards at home. What scars were made in the production and shipping of your food? Which foods have a large impact on the earth? Which have a small impact?

Other Ideas for Recognizing Brokenness

3. Look at the objects around the house. Which objects leave scars when they are produced? Which will leave scars when they are discarded? Consider visiting sites such as a landfills, power plants, or a waste water treatment facility where you can learn more about the scars created by your household.

4. Visit a member of a local environmental organization and ask if there are any local environmental scars. Then visit the site(s). Highways, marinas, airports, and similar projects are possibilities.

5. Remember a time when you hurt the earth. Perhaps, for example, you spilled gasoline on the ground while filling a lawn mower or bought an overpackaged item rather than looking for an alternative. Talk with one another about the balance between assuming guilt for the scars and motivation to take action. We need to recognize the reality of brokenness in our relationship with the earth; yet assuming too much guilt can inhibit us from taking action to change things.

6. Research an environmental disaster such as an oil spill. Visit the site if possible. Consider the immediate damage caused by the accident, and speculate about the long-term effects. Find out if actions have been taken to prevent repetition of the accident.

7. Monitor the newspaper for articles on any new scars that were made on the earth. Create an album of newspaper clippings that appear over a six-month period. Are there any obvious patterns or trends?

8. Write a letter to a company or agency that is creating earth scars (for example, a pesticide company or a company that uses foam pellets in packaging). Cite the effects about which you are concerned and encourage corrective action.

Did you know that an idea that seems right can go wrong? A snowplow was a great help for the snowbound family in this chapter's story, but it left a scar on their land.

Many apparently good ideas have produced long-range scars. For centuries, farmers used a number of natural poisons to protect crops from hungry animals and bugs: lead, arsenic, and copper. In the 1940s, synthetic pesticides began to be produced, DDT first, followed by hundreds of other products.

Every year, American farmers use over 2.5 billion pounds of toxic chemicals on their crops, in addition to the 270 million pounds of pesticides that are sprayed on lawns, trees, ponds, gardens, and parks. The world at large uses 4 billion pounds of these chemicals. The use of pesticides dramatically increased food production, but their detrimental effects on the environment were unknown for years. Rachel Carson noted the effect DDT had on bird populations. Instead of being excreted, the pesticide accumulated in tissues and affected reproductive systems. The birds produced thin-shelled eggs that often were crushed in the nest. Bird populations declined, as few young were produced. *Silent Spring* sounded the alarm on the long-term effects of what once seemed a good idea. Since that time, research has noted the following negative impacts of pesticide use: illness in farmers, rainwater contamination, effects on hormones, genes, and nervous systems, and cancer. Each of these effects has resulted in long-term scars for both the earth and its creatures.

When quack grass was introduced to this continent by farmers, it was believed to be a good cover crop, an aid to sound land management. Today, it is seen as a nuisance species gone wild. Those who introduced it did not know the perseverance and spreading power of this plant as it sprouts white, vinelike runners under the soil. It is almost impossible to stop the spread. Even tarred roads and concrete sidewalks are no match for this introduced species. With the hardiness of this plant, one can realize the damage that has been done to native species.

Some environmental scars are created in the production and use of energy resources: drilling and mining for oil and coal, tapping natural gas reserves, digging gravel from pits to make roads. Environmental impact statements outline both short-term and long-term effects of these operations. But certain effects of their production cannot be foreseen.

The burning of fossil fuels and large-scale forest and grassland burning release carbon dioxide, nitrous oxide, and sulfur dioxide into the air. Acid rain is created when sulfur dioxide and nitrous oxide mix with rain water. The resultant acidic precipitation can damage plants, animals, and fish and can destroy water habitats. Acid rain also eats away stone and metals.

Carbon dioxide, combined with other gases, traps heat in the atmosphere creating a greenhouse effect over the earth. Fifty percent of the greenhouse effect is attributed to the release of carbon dioxide in energy production. Methane production accounts for another 18 percent. Since the last part of the nineteenth century, carbon dioxide concentration in the air has increased by 25 percent. Scientists predict that at these rates, within fifty years there may be a 1.5 to 5 degree centigrade increase in global temperatures. A rise in sea levels, disturbance of marine habitats, dust bowls, extinction of plant and animal species, and dramatic changes in weather patterns may result.

In 1982, a large scar was discovered in the sky. Scientists became aware of a hole in the ozone layer over the Antarctic. Ozone is a pale blue gas that makes up the part of the atmosphere commonly called the ozone layer. It shields humans from the ultra-violet rays of the sun. The scar was created by the production and use of solvents, coolants, aerosol propellants, various plastics, and other synthetic materials. Since the hole was discovered over ten years ago, ozone depletion has more than doubled. The Environmental Protection Agency estimates that a 1 percent decrease in the ozone layer will result in a 5 percent rise in skin cancer in the United States alone. Ozone depletion also affects crops, microscopic organisms, and wind and rain patterns.

As human civilization continues, it is imperative that we recognize the scars we create and the broken nature of our relationship with the earth. Recognition of a problem is the first step toward correction of it.

The Heat Is On: Facing Our Energy Problem by Shelley Tanaka. Illustrated by Steve Beinicke. Buffalo, N.Y.: Firefly Books, 1991.

If You Love This Planet Plan to Heal the Earth by Helen Caldicott. New York: W.W. Norton and Company, 1992.

Resources

The Kids' Environment Book: What's Awry and Why by Anne Pedersen. Santa Fe: John Muir Publications, 1991.

The Spirit of the Earth: A Theology of the Land by John Hart. Ramsey, N.Y.: Paulist Press, 1984.

Earth in the Balance: Ecology and the Human Spirit by Al Gore. New York: A Plume Book, 1992.

Silent Spring by Rachel Carson. Boston: Houghton-Mifflin, 1962.

Magazines:

Earthkeeper: Canada's Environmental Magazine, 11 Oriole Cres., P.O. Box 1649, Guelph, Ontario N1H 6R7.

E Magazine, P.O. Box 6667, Syracuse, NY 13217-7934.

Reconciliation

Become
an
earth
healer.

Healing

The power of healing seems miraculous at times. A child skins a knee, and within a few weeks the wound is gone. Where there was injury, health returns.

Sometimes it cannot return alone. Healers are needed. The earth needs healing. The earth has the healing power of life within it, but sometimes it needs the help of healers.

Read the following story of one earth healer and then look around. Take action. Gain the help of your friends. Become an earth healer.

Everyday Healers

Mark watched as two high school students pulled the last of three canoes up on a rock ledge. It was their third night out in the Boundary Waters Canoe Area Wilderness.

"Carry it over and lay it on that flat area beside the other two canoes," he directed them. "Carry it, don't drag it," he added, hearing the sound of scraping aluminum. This would be the last of these trips for Mark this summer. Mark had worked for a church camp for the last three years. He enjoyed the smaller groups that wilderness regulations now required, although at times he missed the presence of another adult leader.

"This is not just a wilderness trip," Mark told the group as they prepared to leave base camp three days earlier. "This is an opportunity for us to reflect together on life with the earth and with other people. The wilderness will be a tool to assist us with that reflection." That was the way this trip was billed. "Earth Stewardship: A Mission" was the title of the trip in the camp brochure. Mark's job was not only to travel safely with five high school students, but to help them understand how their faith affected their life with the earth and with other people.

"Mark, come and help us pick a spot for the tents." It was Maria, the natural leader of the group. "We found a flat area, big enough for three tents, but it looks like that high area might drain right through here."

Mark walked with Maria toward the flat area. "I've camped here before," he said. "I think we'll be all right if we stay away from the north side of this flat. All the drainage flows there."

As Maria and Lindy, her canoe partner for the day, pitched the tents, Mark returned to the water's edge. Corky and Mike had been joined by Ned, the fifth teenager in the group, and were busily unloading food and gear. "You three are on duty for dinner tonight," Mark told them. "The food is stacked in the side pocket of the kitchen pack. Freeze-dried stroganoff should be on top. The directions for cooking are on the package," he added. There wasn't much that could go wrong with freeze-dried camp food, but Mark had been at this long enough to know that anything can happen when it comes to camp cooks.

A few hours later, stroganoff eaten and dishes done, they all gathered around a fire. The fire circle was a great place for reflective thought and conversation. That night they were talking about earth activism and healing.

"What we need are more Sig Olsons," Lindy said. "He was able to accomplish more by himself than many people combined, and still touch the hearts of people."

"Who exactly is Sig Olson?" Mike asked. "I've heard you mention him several times."

Corky and Ned started to laugh. They couldn't believe that Mike had never heard of Sig Olson. But Maria relayed to the group what she had learned: "He was an environmentalist who was crucial in the protection of these waters. He was a writer, a guide, and most of all a man who was able to share his love of the wilderness with many people. He was instrumental in protecting these waters from motorized travel. He even led the fight to prevent airplanes from flying over the wilderness lakes."

Mark listened, surprised at how much Maria knew about Sig Olson.

"I think he lived over by Ely," she went on. "He has become a kind of hero around here. Lots of people really admire him. I think he died several years ago."

Mark threw another log on the fire. "You know, I met him once."

"It must be nice to have known an environmental hero like Sig Olson," Maria said. The other campers nodded in agreement.

Mark challenged the group at this point. "I think that you have probably known eco-heros in each of your lives," he responded. "They may not have been as articulate and well-known as Sig, but people have been working to heal the earth in many different places and ways throughout the world. I'll bet that we each have known someone who acted out of love and influenced the health of the earth."

They sat in silence for a while, watching the fire, enjoying the rest after a long day of paddling, and thinking about Mike's challenge.

Maria broke the silence. "I don't think I've known anyone who fits your description, Mark. I've lived my whole life in eastern North Dakota, and there isn't much beauty in the earth to love there."

"I've been there, and I agree," Mike said. "That country's only good for driving through."

"I disagree," Mark countered. "I'll bet that some of the farmers in your area can see lots of beauty in the earth, Maria."

"Maybe so," Maria answered. "Even my dad talks about the beauty of black dirt sometimes. I just don't think that it produces any eco-heros."

"I think I've met one, Mark," Lindy said. "A teacher in my school went to the board of education and created a program for all of the fourth graders in the school. They visit an environmental education camp for three days. Everyone learns about the forest environment and all that is needed to protect it."

"That's exactly what I'm talking about, Lindy," Mark added.

"I think the same teacher helped get our school into a recycling program," Lindy concluded.

"Little things like that can cause big changes in the attitudes of people," Mark said as he looked to the others for their stories.

"I read a story once about some people who were activists for the earth," Mike announced. "Our social studies teacher assigned it. I think it was called *The Monkey Wrench Gang*."

"Edward Abbey wrote that," Mark said. "He was one kind of eco-hero. I'd like you to think of some everyday heros, like Lindy's teacher."

"I do think I know one," Maria said, breaking a long silence. "I've known him for years and my dad loves to tell his story over and over again. I just never thought of him as loving the earth." She paused a bit, as if she were reconsidering something she'd known for a long time.

"Well, come on," Corky encouraged her. "If you don't start soon, I'll fall asleep."

"I'll tell it my dad's way," Maria said. "That's the only way that I've ever heard the story of Ole Sundberg. He's in his eighties now. I only know him from church. He always sits in the back row and looks like he's taking roll." She settled back and leaned comfortably against a log. "After World War II, Ole came straight home to the farm. When he returned to our part of the Red River Valley, he was struck by the land as if he had never seen it before. He had grown up there, but his time in North Africa and Italy had given him a new perspective on his homeland."

Maria looked at her group. "If you've never been there you just can't believe how flat and treeless it is. Well, when Ole came home, there were even fewer trees than when he left. His brothers were even farming the land that had once held the house grove. Ole returned in winter, and he was completely depressed by the snirt." Again she looked at the group, asking them, "Do you know what snirt is?" She didn't give them time to answer. "Snow and dirt mixed together and blown into a fine, brown dust that creeps into windows and under doors. Instead of a white Christmas, the valley sometimes has a brown Christmas.

"One day while having coffee in town, Ole heard the county agent saying that the valley was blowing away. The new methods of farming, along with the lack of trees to stop the blowing snow, were causing us to lose our soil. The county agent said that some of the soil blew as far as two hundred miles away. This upset Ole. The county agent went on to say that the only way to rescue the valley soil was to create a system of shelterbelts. The problem was that no one wanted to spend money on trees, and they sure didn't want to waste good farmland growing something that wouldn't bring in any cash. No one, that is, except Ole. That next summer he invested every penny he had saved into buying trees. Within two years, he had planted a row of trees every one-third mile on his family property. There were cottonwoods to stop the wind and pines to hold the snirt. Even people from the next county came driving by on Sundays to see the work of the 'Shelterbelt Man.' It worked. The trees not only decreased wind erosion, the soil retained more moisture because the trees stopped the snow from blowing away. He had to plant a little later in the spring, but his crops were always among the best.

"But Ole didn't stop there. He became a missionary for shelterbelts. He visited Co-op and Farmer's Union meetings. He visited churches and schools. He told everyone about shelterbelts. He even bought trees for people and helped plant them. If you drive through my home county today you'll see a shelterbelt every one-third mile."

Mark, sitting up straight now, responded. "That's a perfect example of an eco-hero, Maria. You don't have to fit any mold. You just have to care about the earth enough to work toward healing it. Here in the woods or in the flat country of North Dakota, it's just the same. Some people who fit the description live in the city. The place is not important. The message is this: love the earth and work for its healing."

Purpose: To educate and motivate ourselves and others by telling stories about earth healers.

Participants: Families, small groups of friends, or a small class (ages eight and up).

Share Stories About Earth Healers

Setting: Any setting will do, but this activity works best if the group has been together for an activity first.

Materials: None.

Spend some time together in an outdoor activity, hiking or playing together. When the energy of the group has diminished, spend some time in reflection about earth healers that you have known. Take turns telling your stories. A story can carry inspiration and truth in ways that no other means of communication can. Take your time. Remember details.

Begin your story with an introduction to the character. Help the listeners feel as if they know the person. Include details that help them know the setting. Try to imagine what inspired the person to do the work for the earth.

Listen to each story. Are there people who remind you of yourself? Is there a similarity between the people in the stories? Are there settings that make it difficult to be an earth healer?

Historically, large movements have been the cumulative effort of many small events. Being an everyday earth healer and telling the stories are all a part of something larger. Tell your stories. And then live them.

Other Ideas For Earth Healing

1. Work as a family to create a land use plan for your yard. Concentrate on reducing erosion from the elements and from human use. Make long-range plans for planting trees and shrubs.

2. Visit local earth healers. Ask them how they became interested in taking care of the earth.

3. Search for a local issue on which to concentrate your own healing work. Remember that the undertaking can be small and still be important to the healing of the earth.

4. Read stories of well-known earth healers. Check the Resources section of this chapter for suggestions.

5. Regularly pick up litter in a local park. Contact your city or county park department for sites that need volunteers.

6. Create a map of your community. Mark the areas that are healthy and those that need healing. Work with your neighbors to restore these areas.

7. Visit an environmental education center or university arboretum. Find out how they are restoring or preserving habitats.

8. Contact The Nature Conservancy, 1815 North Lynn Street, Arlington, VA 22209, to discover areas in your state where land preservation efforts are being focused. Contribute to these efforts.

9. Help young children to heal worn patches of your lawn. Prepare the soil by loosening it with a rake or hoe. Give them seed to spread and help them place stakes and string around the newly seeded areas. Guide them as they water regularly.

**Did You
Know?**

Did you know that you can be an earth healer? Ole Sundberg saw that the land he loved was eroding and found a way to heal it. When the *Exxon Valdez* spilled eleven million gallons of oil in pristine Alaskan waterways, citizens across the United States organized restoration efforts to save the creatures of the sea from the suffocating devastation of a major oil spill.

Environmental restoration, or healing, is a new ecological profession with an ancient principle: to preserve life on this planet. Native Americans lived on this land with a profound understanding of preserving habitats for their livelihood. They used resources carefully, and their activities did not desecrate the landscape for generations. The elders taught the people that they were keepers of the earth, land stewards.

Aldo Leopold is credited with the birth of the land restoration movement in the mid-1930s. He worked with the University of Wisconsin to restore native ecological communities on disturbed land. The Civilian Conservation Corps helped establish what is considered the most extensive collection of restored plant communities in the world. Over thirty distinct community types are preserved in the university arboretum.

The current development in land restoration began in the late 1970s with the environmental movement. By 1988, this prairie- and wetland-focused movement gained national status with the Restoring the Earth Conference in Berkeley, which drew over eight hundred scientists, policymakers, and activists. Restorationists not only heal the earth, but develop an intimate knowledge of the piece of land they are restoring.

People in San Francisco are reintroducing native bunch grass on a rock hill covered with transmitters. The grass was displaced